DON'T
SETTLE

How to Avoid Pitfalls in Your Everyday Life

VERONICA
L. SALTER

All Scriptures in this book have been taken from the King James Version
of the Holy Bible unless otherwise stated.

ISBN: 0615829341
ISBN 13: 9780615829340
Library of Congress Control Number: 2013910300
CreateSpace Independent Publishing Platform
North Charleston, South Carolina

ACKNOWLEDGMENTS

To my heavenly Father to whom I give and surrender "total praise" unto, thank you for allowing me to go through every situation that has caused me to write about it and for the desire to share with others. I bless you, Lord, for giving the ultimate act of love—Jesus Christ, who is my Lord and Savior—to take that which I know I should have received—punishment for my very sins. I thank you, Jesus, for walking with me, for carrying me when I was unable to walk, and for loving me when I was unlovable. I am forever indebted to you, which I will never be able to repay, but I will die trying.

To my earthly father and mother: writing this book has been a joy to my life, and as my parents you both have inspired me in many ways to become the writer I am to bless many others. I love you both greatly and thank you for the sacrifices you've made for us all. I love, appreciate, and honor you both (**Deuteronomy 5:16**).

To my siblings, Carmen, Paulette, and Lamont Jr., throughout all our life circumstances, God has kept us and is keeping us. I pray that you all will continue to trust in the Lord with all thine heart and lean not to your own understanding, but in all your ways acknowledge him, and he shall direct your path (Proverbs 3:5–6).

To my firstborn son, Chadwick, I love and appreciate you greatly. Continue to work hard, set goals, fulfill your aspirations, and thrive with ambition; but most importantly, put the Lord first in all that you do. The Creator of life has your blueprint mapped out for you already. I pray that you continue to ask, seek, and knock for life's answers (Matthew 7:7–8).

To my second-born son, Omar, I am so proud of you in all of your accomplishments. I love and appreciate you greatly as well. I am equally proud of you as you strive for the spirit of "excellence" that I know is in you. Continue to display Godly characteristics in all that you do as a witness for Christ, a light that cannot be hidden (Matthew 5:15–16).

To Pastor Roderick L. and First Lady Pamela D. Hennings of Zion Dominion Global Ministries, Williamsville, New York, thank you, thank you, thank you for being such a man and woman of integrity. Thank you for paving the way and setting an example for so many who have not a clue of your early testimonies of God's grace and goodness in your lives. Truly you both have blessed me tremendously in who you are as servants of God. Thank you for showing me that true, tangible, genuine, earthly love *is* possible. Thank you for every message from 1999–2009 that pushed me to grow, such as "Soul Ties II," April 7, 1999; "An Enemy Has Done This," April 9, 2000; "Bankrupt the Devil," February 2003; and "Restoration," January 18, 2004. Thank you. First Lady Hennings, you are such an inspiration to me. Thank you for showing class, integrity, love, submission, and order. You are truly an "elect" lady. I will never forget the times we shared. They were and still are important to me; we can see much clearer now (pun intended). You are always in my thoughts and heart. Love you all, Arianne, Chloe, and Sandy. You all are true disciples of Christ (John 13:34–35).

To Apostle Robert L. and First Lady Janice Sanders, Greater Refuge Temple of Christ, Buffalo, New York, thank you for welcoming me again and again with arms wide opened. You richly blessed me with the word of God as well as your example of leadership and love. Apostle Sanders, thank you for seeing me as a gift to your son in the gospel, Michael. We love and appreciate you. We pray the peace of God continually rest upon you and family (Philippians 4:7).

To Apostle and First Lady Allen, I thank you for your generosity and multiple acts of kindness. Thank you for welcoming me with open arms into the Christ Bible Discipleship Worship Center family. May God continue to bless you both and enlarge your territories; I pray that his hand will be with you in all things (1 Chronicles 4:10).

Last but definitely not least, to my dearest, wonderful husband, Michael. I love and thank you so much for being you, the powerful man of God has predestined you to be. Thank you for being a loving and compassionate, caring husband. You demonstrate fatherhood like no other; the children are blessed to call you dad. I admire you for the example of Christ you display in your everyday walk. Even as a defender of the gospel of Jesus Christ, I thank you for not compromising. Thank you for teaching the word of God with passion and heartfelt concern for a people and not for any other reason. Thank you for encouraging me to complete this book and set in motion to accompany you in furthering our biblical knowledge and understanding at New Life Theological Seminary, Charlotte, North Carolina. I love you and I look forward to many more years of sharing, laughing, and crying in our growing friendship with one another.

Real love from your,
Dorea

CONTENTS

INTRODUCTION

***Just a thought:* Do you determine your worth by your achievements? Or is your worth settled on who you are in God's eyes? If you answered, "Yes, I am worthy because of my achievements," this way of thinking has to be disassembled. This is considered an untruth that must be dismantled in the mind first.*

Being a woman entails many responsibilities. Female, wife, and mother are just a few to be mentioned. *Webster's Dictionary* describes a woman as the female of a man, which is accurate with the word of God in the book of the Genesis, the beginning, the genes of the world. In chapter two of the book of Genesis, verses 21–23 describe Eve, whose name means life, living as the first woman formed by God out of Adam's side (being). Eve was created, and her role as woman was to emphasize the intimacy, the sacredness, and the inseparability of a God-ordained marital relationship. This relationship would even surpass the parental bond and the connection between mother and child. Matrimony was ordained as ministry. The first ministry, office, or department of the woman was to be to her husband. First Corinthians 11:8 and 9 says, "For the man is not of the woman, but the woman of the man. Neither was the man created for the woman, but the woman for the man." Genesis 2:18 says, "And the Lord God said, it is not good that the man should be alone: I will make him a help meet for him. The woman was created to help the man, her husband, the one who bands her, meet the God-ordained purpose for his life.

From female to woman to maybe a wife or mother are transitions experienced by many women. Unfortunately, all may not have been blissful conversions. In the midst of a woman developing from one stage of her life to another, circumstances happen.

Unfortunately, many women have experienced extreme trauma in their lives one way or another. Some have been molested, raped, rejected, abandoned, beaten, and abused and are still living with the effects of their past experiences. Whether it happened by a relative, a husband, a stranger, or even a spiritual leader, the aftereffects linger into our daily lives whether we want them to or not. That is why we must get to the root of every degrading, demeaning, and shameful episode that has every transpired in our lives. Then we can begin to ask the Lord to sever and detach every act, circumstance, or situation right at the root. We need them to be disconnected and destroyed. The only ways these particular types of wounds, hurts, and voids can be filled are by the love of Jesus Christ, the washing by his blood, and calling on his holy name.

In chapter one, I'll talk about forgiveness. There is a process to forgiving ourselves and also forgiving our minds of every situation that has taken place in our past. We must do this to ensure the behaviors of our past hurts do not spill over into our everyday actions. Women, we can no longer allow grim details of our past to hinder us from moving forward in life. Moreover, our life in Christ is far greater than any accomplishments we could do on our own. It is high time to take our rightful places in this world. Yes! We are in it but not of it (St. John 15:19). God has chosen us out of the world, so the world hates us anyway. Now we must gain our self-esteem back, our self-worth, even the knowledge of being accepted by God, the Father, through our Lord and savior, Jesus Christ. There is no need to be tormented by our past any longer. We are new creatures! (That's what we think! To tell the truth of the matter we are really just fallen creatures pressing to get back in fellowship with God and the predestined place he has called us to from the beginning of creation.) Nevertheless, the old mind-set, the old way of thinking about ourselves, must die. That way of thinking must pass away and be buried, never to be revisited. We must allow all things to become new in our lives (2 Corinthians 5:17). There must be a new way we think about ourselves.

Women, how we think of ourselves must be the way God Almighty thinks about us. God says in Jeremiah 29:11, "For I know the thoughts that I think toward you, saith the Lord," "thoughts of peace and not of evil to give you an expected end." We must also develop a new way we think about those who have wronged us. If God, through his son, Jesus Christ, has forgiven us for the wrong we have done toward him, who are we not to forgive ourselves and those who have "dogged" us, misused us, and abused us? Of course we will not forget all those horrible scenes that sometime replay in our minds, but we can forgive others for initiating them. Philippians 3:13–14 states, "Brethren, I count not myself to have apprehended: But this one thing I do, forgetting those things which are behind, I press toward the mark of the prize of the high calling of God in Christ Jesus."

We must stop condemning ourselves because of things past, yet seek those things that are above (Romans 8:1, Colossians 3:1). The word of God says in Isaiah 54:5, "For thy Maker is thine husband." The Lord is everything we have need of. We must delight ourselves in Him, the Lord, and he will give us the desires of our heart (Psalms 37:4). Once we know who we are in Him we begin to walk worthy of the vocation to which we were called (Ephesians 4:1). We begin to know that we are a "chosen generation," born of a "kingly" nature and a royal priesthood, a holy nation, a peculiar people for a reason. That reason is to show forth the praises of him who has called us out of darkness into his marvelous light (1 Peter 2:9). God chose your gene to be one of his favorites. So, women, *settle no more, accept God's outpour* for your life. We must walk in the intended purpose God has for each one of our lives.

Your question may be, "How am I ever supposed to have a normal life after all that has happened to me over the years?" I am so glad you asked. The chapters ahead will demonstrate the healing power of God in every hurt area of your past, every hurt in your present, and the love of God guiding you by the Holy Ghost (Spirit) into your predestined, divine future.

CHAPTER ONE

FORGIVING YOURSELF! (THIS IS MY LIFE)

**To the Lord our God belong mercies
and forgivenesses, though we
have rebelled against him
Daniel 9:9**

Whenever we hear the word *forgive* we automatically think of the proverbial saying "I'm going to forgive, but I'm never going to forget!" This adage has been used in situations to blame the current hurts of our lives on our past experiences." Of course we will not forget the scars we have, for the scars are evidence of the battle. I say, "Keep the scars, but win the battle!" You win the battle by not allowing that same situation to ever transpire in your life again. 2 Timothy 2:3 states,

*Thou therefore endure hardness, as a good
soldier of Jesus Christ.*

What does it mean to endure? To endure means to suffer patiently or to tolerate something or someone. There are numerous conditions and positions that happen in our everyday lives that are out of our control. Then there are situations we strategically place ourselves in.

As long as we live, many situations will arise in our homes, in the workplace, and with loved ones; however, we must begin to respond to those situations the right way. One of the most important aspects of life is how we respond to them. How we respond is what really counts, and it starts with forgiveness.

If you do not forgive anyone who has performed any evil, selfish, demeaning, illicit act toward you, it will only allow them to have tremendous power over you and your current life. When you constantly remind yourself of those horrific past episodes, you are only giving room and permission for the enemy to work in your mind, will, and emotions—and ultimately your life. This happens all because you did not or will not forgive another.

This only hinders you from moving forward in new relationships. Marital relationship, friendships, business partnerships—all have to be healthy in order for them to survive. They will all become "infected" if we allow old baggage to attach itself to us. We must learn from our past, grow with the scars, and move on. Philippians 3:13–14 states:

Brethren, I count not myself to have apprehended: but this one thing I do, forgetting those things which are behind, and reaching forth unto those things which are before,

I press toward the mark for the prize of the high calling of God in Christ Jesus.

Forgiveness is not for the other person: it is ultimately for you. The Bible says in Matthew 6:12, "And forgive us our debts, as we forgive our debtors." We must pay close attention to the adverb here, *as*. It means to the same degree or amount, equally. So the measure that we forgive others is the same measure our heavenly Father will forgive us, in the same degree or amount, equally. We must be quick to forgive others and not harbor hard feelings within us. Stop what you are doing in the "ministry" and go and get forgiveness right, right away. Otherwise what you are offering is not pure, sincere, or in order with the word of God. Matthew 5:23–25 states:

FORGIVING YOURSELF!(THIS IS MY LIFE)

*Therefore if thou bring thy gift to the altar, and there
rememberest that thy brother hath ought against thee;*

*Leave there thy gift before the altar, and
go thy way; first be reconciled to thy brother,
and then come and offer thy gift.*

*Agree with thine adversary quickly, whiles thou
art in the way with him*

If we refuse to get it right with our brother or sister, it will eventually turn into bitterness, anger, contentions, strife, resentment, and then, ultimately, sickness.

What does it really mean to forgive? What does the word mean? The Greek word for forgive is *aphiemi*. The prefix *Apo* means "from" and *hiemi* means "to send." What this means, therefore, is to send away, the complete removal of the cause of offense, remission of the punishment due to sinful conduct. When Jesus went to Calvary to be crucified, it was the Romans soldiers who were leading him to be put to death.

Jesus asks the Father to forgive *them*, for they know not what they do (Luke 23:34). Here Jesus demonstrates his power in accepting the responsibility of someone else's offense. Jesus asked the Father to send away the punishment due to them because of their sinful conduct. That is powerful. In a sense, Jesus said, "I'll take what they should get instead; give it to me, Father. I'll take the blame." Therefore, we must be willing to forgive other people the same way Jesus forgives us. It does not matter how mistreated you were, how much self-esteem has been ripped out of your life, or how hurt you were—the blood of Jesus Christ, the risen Savior, knows what it feels like just as you do. First Corinthians 10:13 states, "There hath no temptation taken you but such as is common to man, but God is faithful, who will not suffer you to be tempted above that you are able; but will with the temptation also make a way to escape, that you may be able to bear it."

In the process of forgiving others, we must first acknowledge that we are unforgiving to ourselves. It must be recognized that we have not yet found it in our hearts to forgive the offender. Secondly, we

3

must ask those who have wronged us to forgive us for harboring anger in our hearts against them. We must free them, release them, and forgive them. To know for sure that you have done this, the next time you encounter that person, it will be as though nothing ever happened. Although you know that it has happened, you do not charge anything to their account. There is no notable record of the offense. It will never be erased from your memory; however, they are free, with no debt to pay concerning their behavior toward you.

The blood of the sacrificial Lamb, Jesus Christ, is more than able to cleanse every hurt, heal every pain, and turn it into a victorious testimony for someone who must know that God is able. Through Jesus Christ every void can be filled. There may be areas in your life where you think no light could every shine again. These are the dark areas and shallow brooks you may not have shared with any other person. I am here to tell you that no matter how bad it looks or how horrible it feels, the blood of Jesus Christ can penetrate every voided area in your life.

I'm here to tell you that all things are possible with God. So forgive the childhood molester, the neglectful parents, the dishonorable mentors and leaders. You must forgive the violating bosses, the corrupted babysitters, and the unlearned husbands, boyfriends, and pimps; they all must be forgiven.

Oftentimes we are willing to forgive others, but do we really let it go from our own mind? Do you notice there is something holding you back from being all that you can be in God? Ask yourself these questions: Whom have I not forgiven? Why is sickness a part of me now? Holding on to guilt, pain, and resentment for something others have done is only damaging you. I am a witness of this type of behavior. Allow me to share these experiences with you and relate how the Lord helped me overcome the obstacle called "unforgiveness."

I reached a point in my life where I found myself searching for something, but I had no idea what it was. I did not know exactly who I was. I already had a child by the age of twenty-one. I was lost, broken, and out of order, and I did not know it. At the age of twenty-three, I met a man (not Jesus) who took me to a place called church. We were first coworkers at a local factory. Both earning very little at the time, we became interested in one other. Oh, this man was tall, dark, and handsome (to me). He had the charisma of a smooth-talking, get-what-you-want, when-you-want-it, and how-you-want-it con artist. He could talk you out of your last dime if he said it the right way with the right look and that glimmering smile. Needless to say, I was naive, gullible, vulnerable, and *sold*. He had the attention I desired, the look I wanted, and the *God* I did not even know I needed!

There were some things that confused me after the wedding and the baby and giving my life to Christ! The fact that he even invited me to church after the brief dating process was stunning to me. My initial response was, "Church? I don't even own a skirt or a dress, let alone a 'church' outfit!" The best I had was a pair of maroon stirrup pants and a silk cream blouse that I would wear when I went out to the club.

When we dated, I would light his cigarettes, open his "forty-bowl" (forty-ounce bottle of beer), and watch the game by his side—seemed like every Sunday after morning service. The local corner store was always a stop we had to make on the way home from church. This was a weekly ritual. It was not a new hobby; this was normal behavior before and now during the marriage. This was not hidden or disguised before marriage. However, I was not totally ignorant of the concept of church. I thought something was supposed to change after you went. I thought the preacher would say something to make me examine myself to ensure I was doing what the Bible said to do. Well, by the looks of it, this behavior was a "normal" way of living for many in that local assembly, but for me, something changed. I found Christ; it was not just a gathering of people in a building, but deep in the inside of me I noticed my life was about to change. I accepted Jesus as Lord of my life. I realized that I was here on earth for a purpose other than my own selfish motives and desires. My lifestyle, my everyday behavior, even how I talked all began to change. My thought process was unlike before.

So what changed? After eleven years of marriage was dissolved and divorce came into play with enormous amounts of experiential knowledge, I realized the transformation God was doing in my life. After numerous surgeries and sicknesses, I recognized I was holding on to pain, resentment, and anger because I did not forgive when I felt I was treated poorly. Once I reached a point where I had forgiven the committer I wanted to talk to him to see what I should have done better. When asked the questions "what went wrong?" and "what changed?" the answer was, "You did, and I didn't!" I was changing and being modified and customized into the woman God was calling me to be; the committer was aware of the process but was unwilling to change. These experiences are not to be confused with the wonderfully, delightful, God-ordained marriage I have today.

When we allow the word of God to fully operate in our lives despite what we go through, growth is inevitable. In the times when your mate does not come home from work, or when he comes home smelly with vomit and alcohol and you have to put him in the shower because he is too drunk to do it himself, you must know that it is God working through you to get it done. Even when your spouse comes home every week with an excuse about his check and you're left to foot the bill of every expense in the house, including your two young sons, you have no choice but to trust God loves you enough not to leave you in such a situation forever. Most women whose husbands had children with other woman during their marriage are sitting in jail right now or are in mental institutions wondering, "What did I do wrong, or what could I have done better?" Some wives whose husbands went on a one-week cruise vacation without them have been charged with homicide. One celebrated pastor always says, "If you don't wait for God to do it, you're going to have to wait for God to fix it!"(R. L. Hennings) My cry was found in Proverbs 10:22, which reads,

The blessing of the Lord, it maketh rich, and
he addeth no sorrow with it.

So I cried out to the Lord, saying, "Lord, you said in Proverbs 10:22, 'The blessing of the Lord it maketh rich and he added no sorrow with it.' I thought marriage was supposed to be a blessing.

I'm sorrowful down here. *Help me, please!*" I was sorrowful and distressed. Even though I had "placed" myself in that situation, my life was changing. I placed myself in that situation by not taking the proper time and investment to understand what marriage was or was supposed to be. I was just then getting the manual on how to live life through the word of God, and here I was already married with none of the ingredients in the word of God accounted for in my marriage.

I then began to realize the meaning of these words in my life: What the enemy meant for evil, God was turning it around to work out for my good. I was changing, and my vision was coming into clear focus.

I truly believe that whatever we want in our lives, if it lines up with the word of God, he will grant it to us. Deuteronomy 28: 1-68 speaks of "if/then" clauses: If you do this, then I will do that. The marriage was of my own doing. I'll take the blame for putting that thing together. I'll take the blame for having a child out of wedlock, before we were married. Because I did not "Seek ye first the Kingdom of God and 'HIS righteousness'; and all these things shall be added unto you" (Matthew 6:33) was I in a rotten situation. Although I was sorrowful in that place, it was only because I learned how to "delight myself in the Lord" that I was able to continue to praise God in liturgical praise, greet on the hospitality team, and function on a daily basis. I believe if I had not been fixed on the excitement and fascination of my new life, I very well could have lost more than my mind.

Now, let's not get it twisted. I did not know all that stuff before I hooked up with "Mr. I'm sold on your flesh alone." Today, I can truly, sincerely thank God for every negative experience that I set myself up for. Every encounter I have engaged in has allowed me to grow closer and closer to the Lord. I realize that flesh is only a vessel that has the ability to house the true riches of one's being, the Spirit. Paul acknowledged in Romans 7:18 that in his flesh dwelled nothing good.

For I know that in me [that is, in my flesh] dwelleth no good thing: for to will is present with me; but how to perform that which is good I find not.

No matter what we have done in our immaturity, we must find it within ourselves to move past those hardships and avoid making the same mistakes repetitively. It is insane to continue to do the same thing and expect a different result. We must also, as women, begin to speak to our inner selves and say, "I forgive you—now it is time to move forward with life." It is not up to us to try to dissect the past and figure out why something happened to us, what we did wrong to deserve this. Thank God for the grace and mercies he supplied while you were going through your mess. Forgive yourself for allowing yourself to be vulnerable, naive, and taken advantage of. Your forgiveness cannot begin to scratch the surface or compare to the gift that God has provided us through the blood of Jesus Christ. So, tell me, who are you to hold yourself against yourself? God has already forgiven you. Stop tormenting yourself over "your disappointments." So what, you did not live up to *your* expectations. God has graced you to now live up to His. It is time to forgive you and walk in him. Just begin to think about that person or those people who have violated you and begin to pray this prayer:

> *Most Holy Father, in the name of Jesus, I come to you now, from a place I chose to be unforgiving. I am sick inwardly because I have not forgiven someone who has hurt me deeply. Forgive me, Lord, of my every sin of commission, the things I know were wrong, and my sins of omission, those things I omitted to do when you told me. You said that you would forgive us according to the measure that we forgive others in Matthew 6:14–15. You said for if we forgive men when they sin against us, Father, you will also forgive us. But if we do not forgive them their sins, you, Father, will not forgive our sins. I repent and turn from my sins, my wicked ways, and the thoughts I have had toward others. Create in me a clean and pure heart, and renew a right spirit within me, Lord. You said that vengeance is yours and you will repay (Hebrews 10:30). Now, Father, in the name of Jesus, I free, I forgive, and I release all (offender(s) names) _____, in the name of Jesus.*

Amen.

Trust God and be blessed!

Poem

"FORGIVING YOURSELF"

You're So Hard on yourself...
Why is that so?
You have such a hard time
Just letting it go!
Forgive Yourself.
I DID ALREADY—
IS YOUR LOVE MUCH GREATER THAN MINE?
I AM GOD, Sovereign and ALMIGHTY,
MY LOVE IS TRULY DIVINE.
Stop beating yourself up and walk in the place
I have ordained before the beginning,
Just keep the faith and keep in mind
MY LOVE,
It has No
ENDING

NOTES

CHAPTER TWO

ACCEPT THE GIFT

**And not as it was by one that sinned,
so is the gift: for the judgment was by one
to condemnation, but the free gift is of many
offences unto justification.
Romans 5:16**

What does it mean to accept? Well, let us go back to some of our childhood days and see what we might come up with. I believe we all have some tremendous stories we can tell relating to the "good ole' days!" Right? Remember the first gift you received for Christmas as a youngster? It was such a joy to tear up the paper in anticipation of the gift wrapped underneath. You knew it would be something you had placed on your wish list that would bring excitement and fulfillment to your life. You would wonder, "Could it be that sparkling, golden bracelet I have always wanted that symbolized hugs and kisses?"

Perhaps it was that fabulous red sweater you adored in your favorite fashion magazine. The anticipation tended to grow enormously grand as you continued to pass by the winter white–colored Christmas tree. Whatever was housed in the bright, festive, decorated boxes under the tree would be a treat when revealed.

You'd already decided which pair of jeans you were going to wear with your new sweater and also had made certain your nails were freshly manicured to display your bracelet in "excellence." As soon as 12:01 a.m. was displayed on the alarm clock, you and your siblings would beg Mom and Dad to go downstairs to open "just one gift!" With all the "please, Mom" and "please, Dad," they gave in. To your surprise, the sweater turned out to be blue and one size too big, and the bracelet you so desired was a necklace sixteen inches long with rhinestones in it. Although disappointed, you accepted what was given to you because, after all, they were gifts.

To accept means to receive willingly, to agree to, to assume an obligation to pay. A gift simply is something given, or the act or power of giving.

There is a gift that surpasses any gift imaginable. This gift is called the gift of salvation. This gift is free to all but have not been given without a great price. The blood of Jesus Christ was shed for all of humanity, and those who freely receive him as Lord and Savior shall have everlasting life. When you love someone or something, you give to it. St. John 3:16 states:

For God so loved the world, that he gave
his only begotten Son, that whosoever believeth
in him should not perish, but have everlasting life.

For God sent not his Son into the world to
condemn the world; but that the world
through him might be saved.

Love is an action. You cannot say you love something or someone and have no demonstrative activity toward it. Action is a manner or method of performing, the events of a literary plot. God felt something and then did something about it. We must refuse to accept the words "I love you" or "I love that" without a literary plot or an action that proves the statement.

If you love your children, your spouse, or even your ministry, you give your time and attention to it. Usually we give close attention to what we love, and we make sacrifices for it. It would be hard to fathom a new mother who just delivered her first child, whom she says she "loves" with all her heart, turn around and put the infant

12

in a dresser drawer, close it up, and pretend she did not just deliver human life from her body. Anyone in their right mind would not think of doing such a thing. When you see this new form of life, love tells you to feed it, hold it, rock it, change it, take pictures of it, and sacrifice rest to ensure that it is OK. However, there are some stories that seem unrealistic but are all too familiarly true. For instance, a woman from Houston, Texas, by the name of Andrea Yates drowned her five children in the bathtub of their home. Unfortunately, Andrea Yates was not in her right mind. Andrea had suffered for some time from severe postpartum depression and postpartum psychosis. Postpartum depression, also known as postnatal depression, is a clinical depression that can affect women after childbirth. Hypothetically speaking, if there had been no clinical diagnosis for this young lady's actions, there would obviously be no evidence of love shown for those children. These actions display no demonstration of love whatsoever. What I am trying to emphasize here is this—love acts, cares, and responds in a reasonable, rational, and sensible way. It is impossible to say you love and not exhibit it.

The same goes for a "husband and wife" team. It is like a husband who tells his wife, "I love you" day in and day out but never comes home from work for dinner, spends all his money before he gets there, and skips the prepared bath! He misses *all* the kids' events and open houses and "picture days," but he says he loves his wife and kids. Where is the sincere action that makes a statement of his love to his wife and family? The word of God states in 1 Timothy 5:8,

> *But if any provide not for his own, and specially*
> *for those of his own house, he hath denied*
> *the faith, and is worse than an infidel.*

This is worse than being called an unbeliever.

If you love being outdoors in nature—going for walks, jogging, or even bicycling—you spend time in it. If you own a yacht or a ski boat, you go and sail on the water, you have picnics on the shore, and you even take pictures of the sky. These are all relevant actions taken in relation to what we love. We give our attention to that which we love and care for willingly and unselfishly.

So that you too can have this great experience, let us pause for a moment and, for those who have not accepted Jesus Christ as Lord and Savior, let us answer a few questions: Do you believe that God, the Father, gave his only begotten Son, Jesus, to die for your sins? Do you believe that Jesus was born, lived, died and was buried, and then rose again on the third day? *Repeat these words:* "Lord, I am a sinner, and you are the Savior of the world. I repent of my sins. I want you to come into my heart and forgive me of all my sins and cleanse me from all my unrighteousness. I repent and will turn away from all behaviors, circumstances, and people that do not please you, Lord. I confess with my mouth and believe in my heart that Jesus is Lord, and as I yield my life to living according to your word with the sealing of the Holy Spirit I claim salvation and now I am *saved!*"

Congratulations, you have just accepted the Lord Jesus Christ, the most precious gift ever given to mankind—salvation.

The book of Romans describes this wonderful gift given to us who have done absolutely nothing to deserve it. Romans chapter 5:15 and 21 reads,

*but not as the offence, so also is the free gift.
For if through the offence of one many be dead,
much more the grace of God, and the
gift by grace, which is by one man, Jesus Christ,
hath abounded unto many.*

*That as sin hath reigned unto death, even so
might grace reign through righteousness unto
eternal life by Jesus Christ our Lord.*

How much more has our heavenly Father completed such a wonderful *act* for those who would say yes to the precious gift he has freely rendered to us? The gift was without charge to us but was very expensive to the Father to give.

Once you begin to read the word of God and meditate on who he has created you to be, you will not want to go back to those things that you thought would bring you the most joy and pleasure. The drugs only give you a temporary high, and your happiness soon fades away, and you find yourself right back in the same place. The sexual encounters last a much shorter time than the drugs only to leave you feeling worthless and unclean, although your initial intent was a desire to be loved. The pornography crept in to sustain the lustful appetites of both the drugs and sex addictions, but it only leaves you continually wanting more of what you know is morally undignified. Sin will never satisfy. The more you sin, the more you want to sin—always looking for another craving to top off and beat the last craving. How many of you know that you will never find it? Sin is designed as an appetite of indulgence where you only wind up with pseudo pleasure. It is designed to be so enticing to the eye and the flesh that you become arrogant, conceited, and self-important. You put everything else aside because it becomes all about you and your next pleasure-seeking opportunity. Nevertheless, you need to know that this is all a trap for you to stay full of activity for the enemy. It is all a trick for you to stay b.u.s.y.—"Bound Under Satan's Yoke."

God now wants to unlock the gifts he has given you so that he can be made known through you. No longer will you become a pawn in the enemy's hand, destroying the families and lives of so many around you. The ex–drug addict can begin to be an example to those young and old by speaking against the turmoil and havoc that cause his life to swirl into a downward spiral. The ex–sex addict can now counsel the young and the old on the dangers of being promiscuous and all that comes along with such inappropriate, unsuitable behavior. And the ex–pornography addict whose life becomes an open book can become an advocate for the union of marriage and how God created sexual pleasures to be enjoyed by one man and one woman who are married to each other. Here is an opportunity to enlighten others on the ramifications and consequences in the wake of these ungodly behaviors.

You may have great vocal ability or enjoy cooking or cleaning. Look into your inner self and see what brings you enjoyment and delight. What do you always find yourself around? Are young children drawn to you? Do you have a heart of compassion toward young teenage girls? Search your heart and find out what moves you. As you move toward your passions of life, be mindful that your steps have already been ordered by the Lord. Psalms 37 verses 22–24 reads,

For such as be blessed of him shall inherit
the earth; and they that be cursed of him
shall be cut off.

The steps of a good man are ordered by the LORD:
and he delighteth in his way.

Though he fall, he shall not be utterly cast down:
for the LORD upholdeth him with his hand.

Remember, God loves you right where you are but loves you too much to allow you to stay there.

Give, So It Can Be Given

In order to love, you must give. If the Almighty God gave us something that was precious and dear to him, His only begotten—why are we cheapening the gift? Now that the Lord has saved you from death, hell, and the grave, begin to ask God, "What would you have me to do with this life that I now realize belongs to you?" You are no longer your own. You now belong to God, Not Bo-Bo, Junebug, or Jughead. You have been bought with a price. The price of being whipped, spat upon, bruised, and abused is what Jesus Christ paid on the cross for you and me. We can only call him Lord when we ask Him to guide the rest of our lives here on earth. We are truly blessed to have been chosen and loved to the point God gave up such a jewel to see us live. We are walking as gifts from God. Therefore, to defile this gift is like saying, "Please take this ugly, wrong-color, two-sizes-too-big sweater and this necklace I did not ask you for and get them out of my face!" That would be a slap in the face of God. We must not offend God, who gave us the gift of Christ living in our hearts. Romans 12:1 says,

I beseech you therefore, brethren, by the
mercies of God, that ye present your bodies
a living sacrifice, holy, acceptable unto God,
which is your reasonable service.

Beseech means to bid or call forth, to invite or call near. The author of the book of Romans, the Apostle Paul, encouraged them to take heed to what he was saying here. We cannot do any old thing we want to the body God has redeemed unto Himself. God has more for your life than crowding it with nicotine, giving it up for a dinner, or allowing it to be beat on. You are a precious jewel in the crown of His creation. You have been created in the image of God. Genesis 1:26–27 reads,

And God said, Let us make man in our image,
after our likeness: and let them have dominion
over the fish of the sea, and over the fowl of the air,
and over the cattle, and over all the earth, and over
every creeping thing that creepeth upon the earth.

So God created man in his own image,
in the image of God created he him

There is nothing here on earth that has dominion over you. As a creature created in the image of God, you have power, authority, and control over the fish of the sea, the fowl of the air; over cattle you have dominion, and over all the earth, and even everything that creeps, tiptoes, or moves stealthily upon the earth. Therefore, sin shall not have dominion over you. As long as you do not succumb to the devises of iniquity and sin, your dominion will stay in effect. Romans 6:13–15 states,

Neither yield ye your members as instruments
of unrighteousness unto sin: but yield yourselves
unto God, as those that are alive from the dead,
and your members as instruments of righteousness
unto God.

For sin shall not have dominion over you: for ye
are not under the law, but under grace.

What then? shall we sin, because we are not
under the law, but under grace? God forbid.

Your bodily components and faculties have always belonged to God, but once your free will surrendered and gave into the power of the Creator, your body can be used for is glory and His honor. So give your all to the Lord that he will give back unto you.

Delight and Disappointments

Once you accept the gift of salvation, there is a new commandment given unto you. That commandment is found in St. John 13:33–34.

> *A new commandment I give unto you,*
> *That ye love one another; as I have loved you,*
> *that ye also love one another.*

> *By this shall all men know that ye are my*
> *disciples, if ye have love one to another. (KJV)*

Unfortunately, there will be numerous instances where this exact commandment will not be demonstrated by others who steal the title "Christian" in your newfound life. Our words can either bless or curse others. Remember, we are the only beings on earth with dominion, carrying life and death in the power of the tongue. We have a directive to carry out—to love one another. We have to do this always, remembering that Jesus loved us first. Keep in mind where you were when he loved on you. This will be helpful when differences occur, because they will come up.

Allow me to share with you scenarios of what love is not.

Love is not telling a new member (someone who has just given their life to Christ) of your church family, formerly homeless, that she looks like she's going out to the club in the only dress she owns…even if you did not know it was the only one she had. Love is not rolling your eyes because someone else is a size 2 and you're a 22! Love is not ignoring the gifts and talents of a new member because she has not been in your church for fifteen years.

Love would say, "Honey, I have a dress in my closet with the tags on it that I know would look smashing on you—would you like it?"

Love would ask "Ms. Size 2," "Girl, where do you work out? I sure would like to get some of this 'baby fat' off. Would you mind if I joined you?"

To the anointed new member, love would say, "Have you every prayed for someone and they were healed? Sister, do you know what that means?" Well, let me tell you. That is what *love* says and does.

So once you say yes to God, say yes to the blood of Jesus, and accept Him as Lord and Savior in your heart, I beg you to get around those who have accepted the new commandment to love one another as Christ has loved you. There are behaviors that are absolutely unacceptable. If a person cannot add to your life, they do not deserve to be in your life. Whether it is positive influences, words of encouragement, or even just an ear to listen when you need to talk, make sure they mean well and are not self-seeking for their own gain. Get away from those who come just as a distraction or who discourage others to influence your life. Get away from those who come to distract you, those who do not have your best interest at hand and those who are envious of you. You want to surround yourself around those who will love one another despite differences of opinions.

As you walk this Christian journey; there will be many obstacles, especially if God wants to use you to help others come into the knowledge of the truth. So let's go to the throne of God, where he will shield you as he orders your steps in Him.

Prayer:

Most Holy Father, in the name of Jesus, I bless you for changing my heart to say yes to your will and leading me to accept the great gift of salvation. I pray that you help me become focused on you and your work for my life. I surrendered what I thought was my very own life to you. I have given it to you so you can give to me what you desire for this life in you. I ask you for "tunnel vision"—that folly will be far from me as a learn more of you. We bind the hand of the enemy, who would try to choke the seeds that are being planted in my life through your spoken and written word in the name of Jesus. I speak life to every word seed that is attempting to grow in my life. There is no weapon that is forming against me that will prosper, and every tongue that shall rise against me in judgment, thou shall condemn. I decree this to be so in the name of Jesus, I do pray. Amen.

Poem

"ACCEPT THE GIFT"

You accept diamonds and rubies
Houses and cars
But look at where this has
Gotten you so far!

BUT THE TRUE GIFT!

Silver and gold, stocks and bonds
Wealth and riches, knowledge and education…
These are all good; they can place your family
In a safe neighborhood.

BUT THE TRUE GIFT!

The true gift is from above.
GOD gave because of His gracious Love.
To those who take more thought
In the created thing
Instead of the One who gave you your being
I SAY…
Accept the gift of salvation today.
He is the only treasure that shows you the way.
JESUS!

NOTES

_____
_____
_____
_____
_____
_____
_____
_____
_____
_____
_____
_____
_____
_____
_____
_____
_____
_____
_____
_____
_____
_____
_____
_____
_____

CHAPTER THREE

THE STRUGGLE

Put on the whole armour of God, that ye may
be able to stand against the wiles of the devil.
For we wrestle not against flesh and blood,
but against principalities, against powers,
against the rulers of the darkness of this world,
against spiritual wickedness in high places.
Wherefore take unto you the whole armour
of God, that ye may be able to withstand in
the evil day, and having done all, to stand.
Ephesians 6:11–13

Whenever God has a great plan for your life, a plan full of *his* favor, full of joy, full of *him*, you had *better* know that it will *not* come to fruition without a struggle! A struggle, as *Webster's Dictionary* defines it, is making strenuous or violent efforts in the face of difficulties and or opposition. It also means to proceed with difficultly or with a conscious exertion of power.

Case in point: This chapter has been skipped so many times before this book was completed. I have started and stopped for periods too long to even mention. I have lost pages, deleted stuff, crumbled it up, and even completed other chapters—and I still had to come back to "The Struggle!" In the midst of chaos and what I would call "mayhem" in my life, I figured out that it was just another avenue for me to trust, to obey the scribal ministry God had placed in me while working toward the plan and purpose He has for my life. Mayhem is described as needless or willful damage. If we are totally honest with ourselves, we can admit that some of the havoc that goes on in our lives we cause ourselves. Oftentimes we are accustomed to blaming someone else for where we are in life and do not take full responsibility for the actions we have displayed and demonstrated.

It is not always the devil, the enemy, or his imps. Sometimes things happen as a result of our own poor choices and bad behavior. We can definitely be the cause of our own mayhem, creating needless or willful damage in our lives. Maturity leads us to accept what we have done and live with the consequences of our actions.

This is why it is important to keep in mind that despite everything God gives you to build another person up—to inform, educate, and instruct and encourage them in Christ—the enemy will put his best game of distractions out there to slow you down, to make you quit, give up, and forget about it. The word of God says, in Philippians 1:6,

> *Being confident of this very thing, that he*
> *which hath begun a good work in you will*
> *perform it until the day of Jesus Christ*

In this we must be confident: If you have partnered up with those who believe in you and respect you along with those who serve your God and love your Lord, those who pray and pray for others, this is a good start. But most importantly, be confident in the fact that if God gave it to you to do, it will come to pass. Every person has a purpose for being in your life. Whether it is short term or long term, they are there for a reason. They will both build you up and push you toward your destiny, or they will come in your life full of negativity and words that rip you up, tear you down, and not edify you with instruction and improvement. We all should want people in our lives who will make our lives better. It truly becomes a struggle when those who are the closest to you are those who bring the opposition. There are some who will never have an encouraging word, never have anything nice or positive to say about anything or anyone. They always overemphasize and dramatize any and every situation. That is difficult to deal with on any level, but especially when you are doing all that you know how to do to get to that "prepared place" where the Lord has ordained you to be. Paul stated in verses 4 and 5 of Philippians a prayer he prayed with joy because of the Philippians' partnership and labor in the gospel with him.

Always in every prayer of mine for you all making request with joy,

For your fellowship in the gospel from the first day until now

This means he never stopped praying for the people. This demonstrates Paul's concern about the spiritual welfare of the saints in Philippi. We, like Apostle Paul, must continue to pray for each other and support each other! It brought Apostle Paul "great joy" in doing so.

On the contrary, there have been times past when I left the sanctuary after a "high time" in service, where I had received wonderful word, with an uplifted spirit. But before I could get to the parking lot, I had to convince myself all over again that God *has* called me out of darkness—he has washed my sins away; he has chosen me—and that I *was* saved. Why did I have to persuade myself of this all over again, you may ask? I had to do this because, on my course from the sanctuary door to my car, I ran into a whole bunch of people on assignment to distract, dissent, and discourage me. Plainly stated—I ran into some *"haters"* who had absolutely nothing positive, encouraging, or uplifting to say about anything. They were ready and prepared to put a sticky note on my back of what God had delivered me from. They were there to make deposits into my ear gates and live out behaviors that entered my eye gates. Their total mission and assignment, I believe, was to try and snatch the word, the joy, and the encouragement I had just received from the service. It was a distraction aiming to discourage me. No man is perfect, but if the profession of your faith is unto God to live a holy and upright life in his sight, then your lifestyle should also line up. Your speech should line up. Your behavior should all line up with the Excellencies of our Lord Jesus Christ.

Let's define a "distracter" This is a person, place, or thing that draws your mind or attention to a different object. A "distracter" diverts or stirs up or confuses you with conflicting emotions or motives. Have you ever experienced a distraction in your life? They seem to come at the most inopportune times. They come when you are completely focused on an assignment or mission that must be accomplished in your life. Then, out of nowhere, comes something that draws your mind back to something that has *absolutely* nothing to do with the assignment or mission you set out to accomplish. Just imagine, you are *not* thinking about "Brother Work Out," who works out twelve days a week, out of control, like some kind of health nut! But the missionary passes you by in the vestibule and spills into your spirit, "Yeah, if I wasn't married, Sis, I would date him, honey." My initial thoughts were, "First of all, why are you saying what you would do if you were NOT married when you are married?" I was always taught such thoughts should not even pass through the mind of a married woman. Here I am—single, saved, sanctified, sassy, and a self-controlled woman of God—now thinking about what the missionary just spewed out of her mouth. I was hardly thinking about a bicep, a triceps, or any muscle at all at the time of the interruption. This is called a *distraction*! You should run, flee from, and avoid at all costs those types of reactions, especially when the one speaking it into you is unhappy and unfruitful in her own relationship. Our lives must line up with the word of God; before we can speak anything into anyone, we must make sure we are doing it ourselves. We must be very careful whom we allow to speak to us, speak into us, or even speak passing by us. Words are powerful, especially when you are coming into the knowledge of who you really are in God. Guard your heart and guard your spirit. Do not allow yourself to be swayed and won over by the words of others. Stay focused on the word of God. Disallow all distractions that would guide you off course.

Now let us look at another person who may be in your life who has similarities to a "distracter." I call this type of person a "dissenter." This is a person who withholds assent. A dissenter differs in opinion and is not in concurrence with the majority (for whatever reason).

To assent means to agree to something, especially after thoughtful consideration, or to concur. To assent means to consent or agree and concur with what has been proposed. Assent implies an *act* involving the understanding or judgment and *applies* to the propositions or opinions.

Are we taking thoughtful consideration to agree on what is going on in a brother's or sister's life? This is why it is extremely important to welcome the Holy Spirit into your life—he will lead you and guide you into all truth. We do not have to try to do it on our own or take an educated guess and then pray we made the correct decision if we allow the Holy Spirit to walk alongside us.

Just imagine a person who knows God is working in her life. This person went from believing God in areas of her life to knowing that God is already working it out for her good. The only thing she is waiting for now is the manifestation of the promise to come to pass. Then guess who is ready to rear their ugly head? The "dissenter" is standing right at the front door. Here comes the person who wants to withhold assent from what God wants to do in your life. They have concluded with the idea that you were created for them and not for God.

The "dissenter" wants you to do everything for them and them alone. The ideas you come up with to benefit the Kingdom of God through the Lord Jesus Christ are not good enough because they were not theirs. They treat the work God has done in your life as unimportant and meaningless. This is a *dissenter*!

Now, the actions of a dissenter have absolutely nothing to do with your ability to get the job done or your qualifications to do a particular work. This is embedded in the heart of a dissenter. If you could hear their way of thinking, it would sound like this: "If it ain't me, it ain't gonna work, and I will not support it, encourage it, or build it up" (excuse the vernacular). That is a *hater*! The Bible states in Jeremiah 17: 9–10:

The heart is deceitful above all things and desperately wicked: who can know it?

I the Lord search the heart; I try the reins even to give every man according to his ways and according to the fruit of his doings. However, you already know that God has proposed, anticipated, planned, and projected your future. The word of God has confirmed the thoughts he has toward you, telling you of an expected end. But the hearts of the dissenters do not concur with what God wants to do. They differ in opinion and do not agree with what God has already said about you. Dissenters intentionally disagree with what has already been proposed by God. So when consent is not granted at the point where you are, and you believed God had ordained you for such a time as this, just hold on and continue to bless them anyhow. Romans 12:14 says:

Bless them which persecute you: bless, and curse not.

I encourage you to hold on to the promises of God for your life despite the dissenters.

Next we will take a look at the "discouragers." We all have felt disheartened or dejected at some time in our lives. One way we become discouraged for sure is by way of those we have allowed the privilege to influence our lives to begin with. These are people who are not very secure in who they are who we have held in "too high of an expectation." You cannot be discouraged by those whom you prohibit to enter your life's circumference. Be certain those who are in your perimeter have your best interest at heart. A discourager is a person or group of people who rob you of courage or confidence. That is why the Bible says in Jeremiah 17:5,

Thus saith the Lord; "Cursed be the man that trusteth in man and maketh flesh his arm and whose heart departed from the Lord." (KJV)

Please do not put *all* your confidence in someone else lifting you up. Know that all your strength comes from the Lord. God is a jealous God. He will not share *his* glory with anyone. Look at Satan…he'll tell you all about what happened to him when he wanted God's glory. This brings me to another point: Stop asking God for his glory and then not doing anything with it when He shows up. Having God's glory is not just to say you have it or have basked in it. It is to equip and strengthen you to deploy you into nearby and faraway countries, this can be as near as your next-door neighbor and as far away as a foreign country. His glory is to win neighborhoods, communities, cities, and countries to Jesus for the Kingdom of God.

Now is the time to get away from those who distract, those who dissent, and those who discourage. When you become extremely intense about your purpose, you will do something. Change will not come unless you change something. Do not allow yourself to settle for being used by others for their own vain glory or selfish purpose. Desperate measures calls for desperate action. To get something you've never had, you have to do something you've never done (wise words from Dr. Phil McGraw). Get out while you have a mind to make a sound decision.

If we are going to get to where God has called us to be, we must surround ourselves with those who desire the same outcome. Do not get it this twisted. Woman, every man who is placed in your life is not meant to be your husband. Sometimes "Brotha So-'n'-so" is only there to help you and encourage you to be all that you can be in God. So stop being flirtatious, and stop buying monogrammed bath towel (sets) with his initials on them. If you continue to stay prayerful and seek God, he will speak to you during the process. Don't get me wrong—we can still believe God for the desires of our heart. Psalms 37:4 tells us:

> *Delight thyself also in the Lord; and he shall give thee the desires of thine heart.*

Whether you are married, single, divorced, or widowed, I believe many people, especially women, struggle in this area. For example, the struggle of doing things alone, just you caring for the kids, is challenging. You think to yourself, "I didn't make these children by myself; why should I have to bear the brunt of the children alone?" There are many major roles a woman may have to play on a regular basis, which very well could be a struggle to juggle. Let us take a look at them. She is the cook and nutritionist who makes certain her family has a balanced diet. She is "Hazel," the cleaning lady, whose job is to make certain the dwelling quarters are comfortable and clean for the family. Then she is the fitness trainer who has to make sure she stays appealing to the eyes of her husband. Then she turns into "Ki-Ki," the other woman (not literally), who changes her hair and her mood to keep the excitement and fire burning in the marriage. She is the seamstress, the chauffeur the "after-school sporting event cheerleader," the PTA parent, the nurse, the soother, the caregiver; and so on…the list seems endless.

If you are doing these things as a single, widowed, or divorced woman, God will send someone who appreciates the way you know how to "hold it down" in the home if that is God's will and your desire. He will send you someone who values the idea of getting off from work and entering a home and not just the door to a house. Stay faithful and keep doing.

These are all good works. The family is ordained by God. The husband obtained favor with the Lord because he found you.

Whosoever findeth a wife findeth a good thing and obtaineth favor of the Lord. (Proverbs 18:22)

The Bible states that God's thoughts toward us, his creation, are good and of peace, not evil. God wants us to make it. There are some things we must do in order for the promises of God to come to pass. Let us start at denying our flesh. Are we presenting our bodies as a living sacrifice, even in our struggles? Are we coveting the gifts, talents, and abilities in others instead of asking the Lord to develop the gifts, talents, and abilities he has given you? Don't struggle with what God has done in someone else's life. You have no idea what it took for them to be where they are today. They may look as though they have not been through anything. But if you wear a size 10½ shoe, know that you will *never* be able to put your foot in a 5½. When others see where you are, they do not realize you almost lost your mind when your husband went on a weeklong cruise vacation without you when the house note, utility bills, and car payments were all overdue. The size 10½ cannot fathom you wanting to inflict serious bodily harm when you found out that there was another son (Ishmael) who *did not* come from the fruit of *your* loins during your marriage. Not to mention the thoughts of suicide that had to be cast down and denounced because of all the issues at hand. So before you size up your neighbor's shoes and despise God's favor on her life, ask her, "What have you been through to be where you are now?" Before you have outlined a conclusion solely on the outward appearance of another, do me a favor and consider his or her story.

Once you go through your own storm, your own rough places, and your own hardships, you will be that much more graceful and merciful to others before you even know their stories. The key is to keep Christ at the forefront of your mind while you're in your storm!

So when you make it through "that" storm, when you make it through "that" trial with all of its shame, humiliation, and regret, then you can bloom in the "anointing" God will give you on the other side of *your* journey because you did not give up.

Let us pray…

> *Most Holy Father, in the name of Jesus, we come to you now in the name of Jesus knowing that you know the heart of every person. You know our very thoughts before we think them. You know every fiber of our being. Because you are an All knowing and All seeing God, we petition your deliverance and strength in every struggle we are facing. Father, for every struggle we have gone through, are going through, or will go through, we pray that you will give us wisdom in each trial we face. You said in your word that you would never leave us nor forsake us. Help us continually keep our minds stayed on you in the face of adversity. If we do that, we know that we are kept in perfect peace. We pray your comfort will keep us through all of our tribulations according to your word in 2 Corinthians 1:3–4: Blessed be God, even the Father of our Lord Jesus Christ, the Father of mercies and the God of all comfort; who comforteth us in all our tribulation; that we may be able to comfort them wherewith we ourselves are comforted of God. Father God, we thank you for every trial and every struggle. For you said in your word that trials come to make us strong. So, Lord, we thank you for your strength being made perfect when we are weak in the name of Jesus.*
>
> *Amen.*

Poem

"THE STRUGGLE"

You struggle to know who you really are,
Thoughts appear from near and far:
Am I this, Am I that?
How come my eyes were not the ones in which He spat?
Then I would know who I really am—
A royal, peculiar diamond in the rough.
Only He can get me out of this stuff.
It's done, it's finished,
Christ died for your sin.
Now get up and start all over again.
The struggle is over.
It is already done.
Your newness of life has just begun.
You can cast all of your cares
And place them on Him
Because in the end we truly do
WIN.

NOTES

_____

_____

_____

_____

_____

_____

_____

_____

_____

_____

_____

_____

_____

_____

_____

_____

_____

_____

_____

_____

_____

_____

_____

CHAPTER FOUR

"DON'T LET HIM PLAY YOU!"

**The thief cometh not, but for to steal,
and to kill, and to destroy: I am come that
they might have life, and that they might
have it more abundantly.
John 10:10**

For those of you who have surrendered your life to Christ or have rededicated your lives back to Christ in chapter 2, there is more that goes along with your salvation. There is one who comes alongside to lead you and guide you into all truth and to comfort you. St. John 14:15–17 states:

*If ye love me, keep my commandments.
And I will pray the Father, and he shall give
you another Comforter, that he may abide with you
forever; Even the Spirit of truth; whom the world
cannot receive, because it seeth him not, neither
knoweth him: but ye know him; for he dwelleth
with you and shall be in you.*

Jesus was giving instructions concerning the Holy Spirit. As you begin to gravitate to a lifestyle pleasing to God, the Bible shares how we can be led by the Spirit of God. These are called the unctions of the Holy Ghost, the Spirit of truth. This is for the benefit of the believers who love him, which reminds me of the "if/then" instructional clauses found in Deuteronomy 28 describing the promise of blessings and the promise of curses. They illustrate the consequences of following the Word and the mandates of God. If you do this, God is saying, and then I will do that. If you do not do this, then I will allow this to take place in your life. So the condition here is to love Jesus and to keep his commandments. After you have done this, Jesus says, I will pray to the Father, and he will give you another Comforter to abide with you always. In other words, Jesus has your back. He did not leave you hanging or without guidance through your Christian journey.

The Word of God refers to having power after the Holy Ghost comes upon you in the book of Acts 1:8.

> *But ye shall receive power, after that the Holy Ghost is come upon you: and ye shall be witnesses unto me both in Jerusalem, and in all Judaea, and in Samaria, and unto the uttermost part of the earth.*

The Greek word translated as "power" here refers to "freedom of action" or "having the right to act." This is called *exousia*. This includes power to yet overcome all the wicked plans and schemes of the enemy, whose job is to try to hold us back, attempt to seize things from us, and try to strip us of what God has intended for us. His job is solely to steal, to kill, and to destroy. But God will reveal things to us by His spirit. The only way God can reveal anything to you by His Spirit is if you are obeying His commandments and if you love Him. You cannot know the Spirit of God unless His Spirit is in you. In 1 Corinthians 2:12–13 it says,

> *Now we have received, not the spirit of the world, but the spirit which is of God; that we might know the things that are freely given to us of God.*

Which things also we speak, not in the words which man's wisdom teacheth, but which the Holy Ghost teacheth; comparing spiritual things with spiritual.

There is no capacity for the unspiritual part of you—which is your natural, human nature—to receive the gifts of God's Spirit. The natural man is incompetent to the things that can only be revealed by the Spirit of God within us. The Bible calls it foolishness when the natural man uses man's wisdom and education to try to distinguish the things of God. 1 Corinthians 2:14 reads,

But the natural man receiveth not the things of the Spirit of God: for they are foolishness unto him: neither can he know them, because they are spiritually discerned.

The Holy Ghost's occupation is to lead and guide us into all truth. The Holy Ghost will give you "freedom of action" to walk upright in tempting situations and the delegated authority to speak the word of God to weaken and defuse tactics of the enemy against your life.

Once we have realized the power that we possess, we can then be witnesses for Jesus in every region of our lives. In every place you show up, the Holy Spirit will give you what you need to be witness of the transforming work God has done in your life. The power of the Holy Spirit will give you the tools to witness to those you least imagine yourself sharing the word of God with. I believe we all have a relative or friend who has or has had an addiction to drugs. The Holy Spirit in you will strengthen you and instruct you how to share the saving love of Jesus to that "strung-out" cousin, your neighbor next door, your high school buddy in another town, and anyone else you might meet.

Jesus did his part to ensure you were going to be taken care of in his absence from this earth. The gift of the Comforter, the Holy Spirit is yours for the asking, provided your life is in alignment with the Father's commandments and your love toward him is manifest. St. Luke tells us that while we are in the world it gives us pleasure to give good gifts to our children, to lavish them with the desires of their hearts especially when they do something to make the parents very proud of them. In our humanly purest state God sees us as evil people who are trying to do something good. How much more shall your heavenly Father give the Holy Spirit to them that ask him? St. Luke 11:13 states,

If ye then, being evil, know how to give good gifts unto your children: how much more shall your heavenly Father give the Holy Spirit to them that ask him?

If you realize there is something lacking in your life now that you have been redeemed from the penalties of sin, if you love God, and if you are obeying His commandments, then there is much more to obtain in this life as a believer. You now have the privilege to ask your Heavenly Father for the impartation of the Holy Spirit. However, in order for the Holy Spirit to come in and dwell, your temple must be annulled of all sin solely because God cannot dwell in any unclean thing.

In St. John 14:16, Jesus already prayed for another Comforter, another helper who would abide with you forever. Even as Jesus himself was imparted with definite attributes of the Holy Spirit, we are also afforded the same opportunity. The Spirit of the Lord rested upon Jesus. He had the spirit of wisdom and understanding. He possessed the spirit of counsel and might, along with the spirit of knowledge, along with the fear of the Lord.

And the spirit of the LORD shall rest upon him, the spirit of wisdom and understanding, the spirit of counsel and might, the spirit of knowledge and of the fear of the LORD (Isaiah 11:2)

Like Jesus, we too can possess these same attributes. The life-giving Spirit of God can hover over you with the spirit of wisdom and understanding. You too can have the spirit that gives direction and builds strength within you and the spirit that instills knowledge and the fear of God (see *The Message* Bible translation of Isaiah 11:2). Just begin to self-evaluate, to get rid of and eradicate that which is not pleasing to God, which is holding you back from receiving the Holy Spirit in your life.

If the greater one is living within you, possessing such rich and powerful characteristics, there is no reason for you to be fooled, tricked, or deceived again by the enemy. Nothing he does is new. Because Satan wanted to be like God, he cursed himself, and God booted him out of heaven, along with a third of the angels. Even today the devil is continually trying to get glory and praise, not only from the third of his cronies who followed after him, but also from those who are empty and have not asked or accepted the indwelling power of the Holy Spirit. The enemy attempts to destroys these new believers before they to find root in the word of God and before they realize that the Holy Ghost is part of the package of salvation. The enemy hunts for the precious lives only to kill, steal, and destroy those who have been called out of darkness. He will try the same tactics but in different ways. He does the same thing over and over again, each time expecting a different result. If that is not insane, I do not know what is. It even sounds as insane as Satan wanting to be like God, creator of the universe.

So don't let him play you for a fool. Know the game of your enemy, and also know that his plan of action will not work against you! If you can ever entrench in your mind that praises to the Lord Our God will confuse the enemy, you will then praise God no matter what is going on in your life. Here is an example of how praise fights for you. Place yourself in this scenario. You're on your way home after working the midnight shift. You pick your two-year-old son up from the sitter, and you're driving on the expressway. It is dark, damp, and gloomy on the ride home. You coast around the bend of the cold, slick, and icy pavement, and your car begins to spin out of control. The Pontiac Grand Prix does a 180-degree turn in the middle of the highway and is now facing oncoming traffic. Luckily, nothing else is traveling toward you as you remember everything your father taught you about driving in Buffalo's dreadful winter months. Just as you get the car facing the proper way, you see the early morning traffic quickly approaching in the rearview mirror. When this happened to me, I began to shout praises to God at the top of my lungs while the baby was still sound to sleep in his car seat. It was a victory, and at that very point of triumph I began to yell praises to the Lord in gratitude and thanksgiving for the protection he provided. However, after experiencing something so devastating, I know some who would have become paralyzed at the thought of driving again, let alone even stepping foot in an automobile ever again. This incident could have allowed fear to set in. I quickly realized this was an opportunity for the enemy to use this episode against me. I knew God has not given us the spirit of fear. 2 Timothy 1:7–8 reads,

> *For God hath not given us the spirit of fear;*
> *but of power, and of love, and of a sound mind.*
>
> *Be not thou therefore ashamed of the*
> *testimony of our Lord.*

The enemy would try to use this incident to make you become paranoid about ever driving again so he could then smother your growth and progress in the things of God. He would then try to have you to operate in the spirit of fear instead of in the power of God with soundness of mind and a spirit of love. But we know that the devil is a liar and a defeated foe. Sometimes the Holy Spirit will give us an intense desire to praise God at (what we may feel is) the most inconvenient time. If we are obedient, it will be revealed to us why it was imperative to give God praise at that particular time. You may drive about five miles up the road and see an automobile flipped over and four kids standing on the side of the road with their injured father cradling each of them in his arms. There are times when we must send the praises unto God and let praise fight for us. When we praise God in the midst of the storm, we will win every time. I challenge you to shout to God with a triumphant voice of praise the next time you get some disturbing news or are in a situation where you have no idea how you got there or how you are going to make it out. Some may look at you strangely or even call you crazy, but know that your crazy praise is working on your behalf.

When trials come, our natural being tells us to sulk, cry, worry, and have a pity party about what just happened. Some begin to murmur and complain about the trial instead of seeking God in regard to what is going on and what you as an individual can do to correct it. There is a greater one in the inside of us that will tell us what to do at the very moment of uncertainty.

So do not allow the enemy to play with your mind when things are going amok in a violent, frenzied, or uncontrolled manner. He wants you to lose control and do irrational things. At these points in life, he would love for you to engage in unreasonable thinking and have an emotional, knee-jerk response to the test. These are the opportunities the devil would like to use against you to ruin your testimony of the work of Christ in your life. But *do not let him play you* like that.

Here are three facts you should know about any hardship or test that will come your way.

> #1. The trial is coming. PERIOD.
> #2. Trials come to make you strong.
> #3. You must praise God *in it*!

One of the first critical facts to be mindful of is to know that the trial is coming. Even if you are a good person doing everything in your power to do the right thing in life and the right thing to everyone you come in contact with, you are still going to be faced with trials. The tactics of the enemy do not stop just because you perceive yourself to be a good person. Jesus was a good, Godly, holy, helpful carpenter as he walked this earth—100% man as well as 100% God. You can be saved for one hundred thousand years and give to every charitable organization on earth and gladly give your tithe to your church affiliation along with hefty offerings and have fifteen fruits of the spirit…I guarantee if you say yes to Jesus, you will still have to face a test of stamina through subjection to suffering or temptation. No matter how wonderful you are, you will still have to deal with sources of vexation or annoyance in your life.

Now that it is clearly understood that no one is exempt from going through an assessment of fortitude, let us examine how to become triumphant through it. At this instant you are aware the trial is coming, and you will be expecting it. Now you should not be thrown off guard when it comes. Look at it this way: You have placed an online order and are waiting for the package to arrive on the estimated date. You know you placed the order, you know which credit card you used, and you even have a confirmation number. We must do the same thing with the tactics and plans of the enemy, especially after experiencing other victories in Christ. God may have delivered someone you had been praying for or allowed you a promotion on your job. Or God may have healed a loved one from a debilitating disease, whatever your praise report, look at it as an opportunity for the enemy to try to come in to discourage you. He will try and raise his ugly head to attempt to kill, steal, or destroy the joy and enthusiasm you have just gained from the miracle and victory from the Lord. Please celebrate and give God the glory for what he has done. Tell everyone you know that God is a healer, a deliverer, and a provider. However, do not celebrate so blindly and intensely in the victory that you never see the devil coming. Stay focused and on top of the enemy's game so that you will continue to be able to defeat his tactics and strategies.

Secondly, trials come to make you strong. They come to solidify your stance in Christ, to make you firm, solid, and sturdy. They come to test what you are made of. If the enemy had any say so in our trials, he would say things like this to God, "Can they still give you praise in this?" "Will she continue to sing praises when she just got fired from her place of employment?" "Can she continue to be focused on serving on the finance committee when she knows her husband is cheating on her?" "That is nothing to praise you for. I bet I will get her on this one." "How much will she praise you when she finds out her husband may have been violated by another man?" All these irregular and unexpected changes are enough to cause you to question if God even knows what is going on in your life or if He knows that you even exist. But as you continually praise God in it you will get stronger and more firm in God. God's word will became real to you in the time it seems thought He is not near. He will show himself mighty and show you that He is with you and have no plans on forsaking you. God will prove that He is with you no matter what you are going through.

The third point you should remember when going through hardship and tests is that you must give thanks and praise right in the middle of your trial. At the very point when you are confronted with that affliction or heartbreak began to praise the Lord like you have lost your mind! You will win every time. That trial will not seem as bad, nor will it last as long as you anticipated before you praised him. In all things, give thanks. Paul said, I have learned to be content in whatsoever state I am in Philippians 4:11.

> *For I have learned, in whatsoever state*
> *I am, therewith to be content.*

Apostle Paul was saying that no matter what was going on around him, he was able to become undisturbed and still and content. This contentment only comes with practice. How can we learn, become skilled, or gain knowledge on how to be content or at ease if we do not rehearse praise in trying times?

Giving thanks always for all things to the Father in the name of our Lord Jesus Christ is what we are expected to do. The Spirit of God will make it possible for Christians to be grateful for all things divinely allowed to enter their lives. Satan had to get permission from God to work a number on Job because Job was an upright man who loved God and shunned evil. God will definitely work it out for every believer who does the same. He works it out for our good, whatever it is we are going through. Romans 8:28 states,

> *And we know that all things work together for*
> *good to them that love God, to them who are*
> *the called according to his purpose.*

Please do not misunderstand me. None of these sufferings feel good, nor is it by any means easy to praise God when we feel bad. Nevertheless, it is imperative for us as born-again believers, new believers, and *seasoned* super saints to continually be filled with God's Holy Spirit to be led and guided throughout all situations.

*** Newsflash***

It is OK if you have been in church for over fifteen years to get a refilling of the Holy Spirit of God. If a brand-new car with a full tank of gas cannot last fifteen years on the same tank, what makes a person think he or she can? When Jesus bought our souls with is redemptive blood, He did it once but for all. We do not have to accept the Lord Jesus Christ as our Savior every week in order to be saved week by week, but we do need some more gas in our spiritual gas tanks to keep us going from week to week, month to month, and year to year. Who told the saints of old that once you hit the fifteen-year mark of being a Christian that you had no need to be taught anymore or that you could not learn anything from anyone who had been in church fifteen years or less? Who told you that you did not need a refilling or a refreshing of the Holy Spirit of God? New converts are not the only people allowed at the altar. Every Christian can use another touch from the Holy Spirit, and as long as we are alive, we all have something in us that needs to die daily (bad attitudes, distrust, and anger, just to name a few). Please, always remain faithful and teachable. Please know that there is always something someone else knows that you do not. We can even learn a lesson from a talking donkey if we stay teachable.

Praise is not predicated off your feelings. It does not matter how you feel—you have been commanded to praise the Lord. This decree does not state to extol, honor, and praise the Lord only when you experience great pleasure and satisfaction. There are numerous scriptures pointing us to praise as a command and not an option. Here are a few: Psalms 116:19, 150:1 and 6, 117:1 and 2, 135:1, 3, and 21; Isaiah 12:4, 25:1, 62:9; Joel 2:26; Romans 15:1. His thoughts toward us are not great distresses or misfortunes. God wants to give us our expected end (Jeremiah 29:11). When we constantly put these thoughts and concepts of the word of God in our heart, it will help us recognize the tactics of the enemy, who tries to throw us off point. The power of the Holy Spirit will not allow us to be played like the devil's fiddle.

We know that the word of God says, "Faith comes by hearing and by hearing of the word of God" (Romans 10:17). I previously listened to a message about "Marrying yourself to dynamite."

What the message conveyed was this: Marry yourself to TNT. Become one with your "Trials and Tribulations." If you become one with your trials and tribulations, as you do with a spouse, you have to know first of all that your spouse is coming home, as is your trial. Then you have to be wise enough to know which words to put on it when it comes through the door, like your spouse coming home from a bad day. When we said yes to Christ and allowed him into our hearts, we also said yes to long-suffering as when we said, "Till death do us part." So what am I talking about here? Let us take a look at dynamite.

Dynamite means of or relating to physical force producing motion. When your trial or tribulations come, you will either fight or take flight, being mindful that your struggle is not a matter of flesh and blood but rather a matter of spiritual evil coming against the purpose God has for your life.

Ephesians 6:12 reminds us of this very thing.

For we wrestle not against flesh and blood,
but against principalities, against powers, against
the rulers of the darkness of this world,
against spiritual wickedness in high places.

Do not allow your tests to make you flee from the will or presence of God. Do not allow yourself to get so bummed out about what is going on that you stop everything around you until it passes. It may never pass if you do not take any action against it. There is always something to be done on your part when going through a storm. Remember, dynamite is of or relating to physical force producing motion. There has to be a potent energy and strength to drive the negativity away. So it is very important to stay focused, calm, and in a great place of peace to determine what type of force you are contending with. Also, refrain from being moved by your emotions and feelings. Acknowledge the trial or test, but do not respond out of ignorance, not knowing what you are up against. Allow yourself some quiet, decision-making time. Once you do that, you can react as though you knew it was on its way. For example, say your husband pulls into the garage after a long day's work, and, before you see him, you hear the car door slam as though the hinges came off. You then hear the cat let out a loud, scratchy screech as though in pain from some mishap. Finally, as your husband enters the kitchen door leading from the garage, you observe a huge coffee stain on the brand-new blazer you just purchased for him. So, ladies, by now you should have gathered enough information to indicate how his day went without him uttering a word. Although common sense is no longer common, it would tell you now is not the best time to tear in to him about the laundry bill being fifty dollars more this month as opposed to the last two months. Nor is it the right time to talk about packing or painting the new hole appearing in the kitchen wall from repeated door slams.

You must now determine which type of force you should use against the enemy who has been eating away at your husband all day. You must now strategically plan out how you are going to get rid of the wile and tactic that the devil has used against him throughout his workday. Whether it is prayer intercession, the spoken word of God, or the blood of Jesus, someone has to create physical force producing motion to rid the devices of the enemy.

What type of force do you use?

Therefore, we must remember what 1 Peter 4:12–13 speaks of. It reads as follows:

Beloved, think it not strange concerning the fiery trial which is to try you, as though some strange thing happened unto you:

But rejoice, inasmuch as ye are partakers of Christ's sufferings; that, when his glory shall be revealed, ye may be glad also with exceeding joy.

Do not think that because you are saved, because you love God with the possibility of being filled with the gift of the Holy Spirit that you are not going to have any adversities, hardships, or misfortunes. I dare say, perhaps because you are saved and love God is the reason you have heartbreak, grief, sorrows, persecutions, and people who wrong you. Instead, we must rejoice inasmuch as we are partakers of Christ's suffering. So don't let the devil play you. Recognize the signs that alert your spiritual radar.

Now that you recognize that the enemy is going to try to show up after your victories, just begin to place in your mind at that very point of victory a quick "snapshot" of someone, something, or some situation trying to come in and kill, steal, or destroy your success. You then must place the Word of God on it immediately so whatever the enemy planned will not manifest. "No weapon that is formed against thee shall prosper and every tongue that shall rise against thee in judgment thou shall condemn" (Isaiah 54:17). And it shall come to pass (Deuteronomy 28:1); All things work together for the good of them who love God, to them called according to *his* purpose (Romans 8:28); I am the lender and not the borrower (Deuteronomy 28:12); I can do all things through Christ who strengthens me (Philippians 4:13); Nothing shall separate me from the love of God (Romans 8:39). But my God shall supply all your needs according to his riches in glory by Christ Jesus (Philippians 4:19). Get the word in your heart to combat the enemy. If you cannot find it in the Bible right away, write it on the tablet of your heart, memorize it, and buy a concordance so you will be equipped to find it when needed. The enemy does not care if you quote the chapter, verse, division, number, and book, the Old Testament or the New Testament. *He does not care!* Quote all you want. The enemy just doesn't want you to speak it and live it, too. When you speak it out of your mouth and live it in your everyday life, that is power enough to make him flee. The word of God is power, and it is truth. The enemy cannot stand in the face of truth. Hebrews chapter 4:12 states,

*For the word of God is quick, and powerful, and
sharper than any two-edged sword, piercing even
to the dividing asunder of soul and spirit, and of
the joints and marrow, and is a discerner of the
thoughts and intents of the heart.*

God's word will not return unto him void. It cannot. Isaiah 55:11 says it will accomplish that which it set out to accomplish. Some people may think you are not "saved" enough until you can memorize every verse in the Bible that you need in any situation. This is so not the truth. As long as you put God in remembrance of what He has already spoken and declared, God has an obligation to fulfill his Word. In Isaiah 55:10–11 the word of God states,

*For as the rain cometh down, and the snow
from heaven, and returneth not thither,
but watereth the earth, and maketh it bring
forth and bud, that it may give seed to the sower,
and bread to the eater:*

*So shall my word be that goeth forth
out of my mouth: it shall not return unto me void,
but it shall accomplish that which I please,
and it shall prosper in the thing whereto I sent it*

What I perceive God saying here is this, "The same way I have commanded the rain and the snow to come from heaven with a specific task to water, lubricate, and make moist the earth to produce flowers and harvest, this will be the same thing that happens to you when you speak my words back to me." God has a purpose for His word—spoken, lived out, and demonstrated. What is important is that you know it, you speak it, and you live it, and it delivers you out of your situation and circumstances. In addition to studying the word of God, this will give you much more ammunition to combat the trickeries and scams of the enemy.

God has given women, particularly, permission to be totally disturbed and annoyed with the devil. He has granted women an "irreconcilable hatred" toward the devil. Genesis chapter 3 verse 15 states,

*And I will put enmity between thee and the woman,
and between thy seed and her seed; it shall bruise
thy head, and thou shalt bruise his heel.*

There is a spiritual barrier between the woman and the enemy. The word *enmity* means to have an unpleasant will toward—mutual hatred, animosity, and hostility. We have every right to hate the devil because of his deceitful ways. We also have to be a "tad bit" ticked off with Adam for not being close enough to cover us. Eve was not created when the instruction was given to Adam. God spoke to Adam (the man) in Genesis 2:16–17, commanding Adam which trees he could freely eat of and which were forbidden him.

*And the Lord God commanded the man, saying, Of
every tree of the garden thou mayest freely eat:*

*But of the tree of the knowledge of good and evil,
thou shalt not eat of it: for in the day that thou
eatest thereof thou shalt surely die*

Eve was not taken from Adam's rib until after he gave names to every living creature, the fowl of the air, the cattle, and every beast of the field. There was not a helper yet created comparable to him. In Genesis 2:21–22 is when Eve was created after Adam was given the command.

*And the Lord God caused a deep sleep to fall
upon Adam, and he slept: and he took one of his
ribs, and closed up the flesh instead thereof;*

*And the rib, which the Lord God had taken from man,
made he a woman, and brought her unto the man.*

So, women, we must be ready to combat the very thought of the enemy every beguiling us again. Beguile means to deceive, to reason falsely, to catch by bait. Familiarize the signs of being played so that you will never get played by the devil again. He is sly, sneaky, deceitful, cunning, and a liar. He will take what is true and distort, twist, and change it for his benefit. I stress the fact, women, to talk *only* about that which you have factual information. State the facts, and do not be as the master deceiver by adding anything to the facts. Submit to someone who is totally submitting to God. Not halfway, not following half the instructions or three-quarters of the instructions God is giving him, but someone who has completely and entirely submitted to God and His commandments. This was the very first role reversal in the Bible. Adam listened to his woman instead of obeying His God.

Food for Thought

Could it be that Adam did not communicate to Eve what the Lord God commanded him about the tree of knowledge of good and evil? Was Adam not close enough to secure Eve from the dangers of the Satan? That's another book.

The prayer:

Heavenly Father, in the name of Jesus, we acknowledge you as the creator of life. We pray to you today because you are the answer to life. Father, you are the one I can turn to when it seems all hope is lost. You know everything I am going through now, you know everything I have already been through, and you know what I will go through in the future. I examine myself and ask that you remove every hindrance in my life and in your way that will disallow your Holy Spirit to dwell with me, in the name of Jesus. Cleanse this temple that you will be pleased to inhabit so I can be led and guided by your Spirit in all that I do, say, and think.

I ask you for wisdom in the name of Jesus. You said if any man lacks wisdom, he can ask you for it, Father. I pray that for every trial I will encounter, you will endow me with the wisdom to react the way my Savior Jesus Christ reacted. I pray the Holy Spirit will bring back to my remembrance the word of God to use in every situation I encounter and that I will use the word of God skillfully to defeat the tactics, strategies, and schemes of the enemy. Thank you for not leaving me comfortless and for being with me always. I curse the works of the enemy and render them powerless over the lives of every believer reading this prayer, in the name of Jesus. We give you thanks; we honor you and praise your Holy name. In the matchless, wonderful name of Jesus we pray. Amen.

Poem

"DON'T LET HIM PLAY YOU"

He played you, She played you, and
They did too
To the point you thought there was nothing
Else you could do.
They fought you, they ripped you,
And kept putting you down,
Until one day you realized
You've been leveled to the ground.
You expect this from Satan, for that is his job to do
But not from those who should have been the closest to
you.
To free and forgive releases you
To the call God has predestined you to do.
Now that you know, you pray and move on—
God has great plans for your future and beyond.
It's called eternal life
As long as you stay in Him…
Stay the course, keep the faith,
Never give up running the race.

NOTES

_____
_____
_____
_____
_____
_____
_____
_____
_____
_____
_____
_____
_____
_____
_____
_____
_____
_____
_____
_____
_____
_____

CHAPTER FIVE

THERE IS "SAFETY" UNDER THE BLOOD

**But if we walk in the light, as he is in the light,
we have fellowship one with another, and the
blood of Jesus Christ his Son cleanseth us from all sin.
If we say that we have no sin, we deceive
ourselves, and the truth is not in us.
If we confess our sins, he is faithful and just to
forgive us our sins, and to cleanse us from
all unrighteousness.
1 John 1:7–9**

Have you ever experienced your sins lived out again by someone who thought it was important to tabulate them in his or her pocketbook or wallet? Have you ever talked to certain people and noticed the only conversation that ever comes up is about *your* disgusting past faults, failures, and transgressions? Has anyone every greeted you with a sticky note full of reminders of what you used to be and the very wicked place God delivered you from?

These situations are real, and they happen to people like me and you every day. This may be one of the reasons why churches today are like revolving doors because of those who inaugurate themselves as record keepers of everyone else's ungodly behavior in order for theirs to go unnoticed.

These types of behaviours are conveying destructive messages. It should be more apparent that Christians today are more for your deliverance than your bondage. It should be the Christians' desire and pleasurable satisfaction to see someone who once struggled with the entrapments of the snares of the enemy become loosed and set free from the bondage of sin. The Bible says that we should rejoice in the Lord always; Psalms 105:3 states,

Glory ye in his holy name: let the heart of them rejoice that seek the Lord.

If the angels in heaven are rejoicing over every single soul who comes into the Kingdom of God, who are we to hold back our praise to God for those who seek newness of life? The heart of the Christian should rejoice at every soul that gives his life to Christ. The question today is this: Are Christians in today's church excited enough when lost souls are won over to Christ to the glory of the Father? Or are today's Christians afraid new converts will put them out of a "position" in the church. Or will their zeal and passion for their new life in Christ supersede those who have grown lukewarm? "Seasoned believers" should know that no servant is ever greater than his master. What is a "seasoned believer"? I think of this person as one who has excitement, flavour, zing, colour, zest, and pizzazz for the things of the Kingdom of God. However, the season must stay fresh enough that the long-standing believer does not become suspicious of new converts who have the same passion once afforded them in the beginning stages of finding the Lord. St Luke 6:40 says,

The disciple is not above his master: but every one that is perfect shall be as his master

The mature believer who has evolved in Christ has much more knowledge and wisdom enough to entreat the "new" convert as an apprentice. Their seniority and authority should not be used to belittle and degrade new converts for where they have been. As long as the trainer has experience, the apprentice will always give credence to the instructor. The student can never be above his teacher. The student can have the propensity to be like the teacher, but never will he be above his instructor.

The common goal now is striving as children of light, sons of God, and joint heirs with Christ. The aim should be to become leaders who create disciples and leave legacies. A good leader always endeavours to work out of a current position to prepare his disciples for future promotion.

No one has the right to hold another's blood-washed sins and iniquities against that person. There is no variance in the blood of Jesus. There is not a concentrated blood for those who have been saved fifteen years or more and a watered-down, diluted blood for those with only fourteen years or less of salvation experience. There is no seniority in the blood. It is a dangerous thing to keep record of your neighbors' shortcomings as though you never needed God's grace and mercy. We must keep the blood of Jesus "fresh" in our own lives, and then we will not have time enough to worry about someone else's "*stuff.*" Can you imagine the Lord (if you are allowing *him* to be Lord of your life) putting billboards in your face every hour on the hour of every sin you every committed and then telling you about it? No. God is a forgiving God, a merciful God. He has excused and pardoned every sin committed. So if this is you I am talking about, I command you to *stop it*, in Jesus's name.

Who made you the *ultimate* "Christian monitoring technician"? Sin is sin, and the blood is the blood. Regardless if you are a liar, a fornicator, an extortionist, or a murderer, they are all against the word of God. As for a fornicator, the word of God tells us to make a conscious decision to present all of our faculties, body parts and every member of our bodies a sacrifice to Him. By doing this we give onto God spiritual worship *(Amplified)*.

> *I beseech you therefore, brethren, by the mercies of God, that ye present your bodies a living sacrifice, holy, acceptable unto God, which is your reasonable service.*

If someone has committed to presenting themselves sacrificially, living holy for the Lord in all that he or she knows, do not condemn them anymore. This is the true and proper worship that is rendered to God. The word also tells us in 1 Corinthians 7:8–9,

I say therefore to the unmarried and widows,
it is good for them if they abide even as I.

But if they cannot contain, let them marry:
for it is better to marry than to burn.

If the passions of the unmarried and the widows are overbearing, it is better for the man to search out for his good thing and the widow to make ready for her spouse. In regards to the extortionist, the embezzler, one of the very Ten Commandments tells us not to steal in Exodus 20:15.

Thou shalt not steal.

It is not a good thing to covet or crave what belongs to someone else. Could a covetous person desire something someone else has so excessively that he may want to murder another for it? Just as Cain was envious of his brother, Abel, in the book of Genesis chapter 4 verse 8, his wicked heart caused him to react to the iniquity in it. It was because Abel offered the much better sacrifice. Does your envy and jealousy of another strike up enough anger to cause you to kill someone? Do not allow deep-rooted anger to store up in your heart. Strangely enough, this is done every day with the words spoken against others. But as blood-washed believers, you do not have to settle for idle, vain, death-embracing words by others. You can combat them with the word of God. You now have the liberty and the power to accept or decline what you hear. The Bible tells you to try the spirit and see if it is of God (1 John 4:1). (Note: It does not read: "Try the spirit by the spirit." Please read it again and quote it correctly.) If it is not written in heaven, you can bind it up and untie what heaven has said about you and not accept what did not come from God. Do not get bent out of shape because someone else already has something you desire. The word of God clearly lets us know that envy should not be in our hearts, for there is no respect of persons with God. He chooses whomever he wants to and uses them however he wants to. (Romans 2:11, Acts 10:34, 1 Chronicles 19:7). So stop whining and crying about Sista Soldier and Brotha Do Rite and begin to seek the Lord because you love Him and are grateful to Him, and He will then also give you the desires of your heart.

You must continually thank God for the blood of Jesus. Thank the Lord for caring enough about you to give you the blood of Christ to cleanse your mind, your thoughts, and your actions and forgive you for your bad behaviors.

There is no human man's blood alive today strong enough to save, set free, or deliver. That was Jesus's job. Human blood does not have the concentrated ingredients to cleanse something as dark and black as coal or soot—as our sins were. The word of God says in Isaiah 64:6,

But we are all as an unclean thing, and all our righteousnesses are as filthy rags; and we all do fade as a leaf; and our iniquities, like the wind, have taken us away.

But we are all as an unclean thing. There is nothing righteous about us outside of the blood of Jesus. The word of God says, "We all have sinned and fallen short of the glory of God" (Romans 3:23). We do not have the power to make whole, to clean up, or to set free. How can we clean anything if we have the need to be continually cleansed? *Only* God can cleanse and make whole. Through the perfect sacrifice of the blood of Jesus Christ all our sins have been washed away. So to think of yourself above what you are is meaningless, worthless, empty, and vain.

The blood of human beings is a red liquid substance that circulates to the heart, arteries, and veins. This creates a bloodstream that flows throughout our circulatory system. The blood's general functions are to transport, regulate, and protect. It is the fluid of life. Without this fluid there is no lifespan or lifecycle of the human being. It delivers essential elements like nutrients, gases, and hormones and transports waste products. In a single day, the heart of an average adult pumps the body's blood supply of approximately five quarts, which is about 8 percent of our body weight.

There is arterial blood, which is bright red because of the lesser amount of oxygen it contains opposed to the venous blood, which has a darker, dull red color—it needs more oxygen to supply to most tissues in the body. Although there are different indexes of blood inside us, our blood does not qualify as able to purify. Only the sacrificial blood of the Lamb of God qualifies to purify. How has the blood of Jesus translated your life into something new? Do you remember the drug and alcohol lifestyle you used to live? Do you remember the place of loneliness that caused you to fill the void in your life with men? You remember those bad behaviors and sickening habits you indulged in before the Lord changed your life around. There may be some who are in the middle of their transition even while reading this book.

As you recall how you were renewed and transformed by knowing that the blood of Jesus Christ our Savior changed you from what you use to be into what God will have you be, you must also be patient with those whom God, through the blood of Jesus, is still converting.

In this time of change, there is safety under the blood of Jesus to regulate your mind. God wants to govern and direct you according to His rule. He wants to put your mind back in "good" working order. The word of God states in Isaiah 26:3,

Thou wilt keep him in perfect peace, whose
mind is stayed on thee: because he trusteth in thee.

You must continually bless God for not allowing you to be consumed by your prior drug use and alcohol abuse. Thank God for protecting your liver and your brain from being totally destroyed. Because you now acknowledge that it was *only* the grace and mercies of God that kept you when you did not know you had a need of Him. The Lord will allow certain things to happen to you when you do not acknowledge Him as the Most High, Holy, and Sovereign God. In Daniel 4:35–37, King Nebuchadnezzar's sanity was restored to him only after he lifted up his eyes toward heaven and recognized the rights and authorities of God.

And all the inhabitants of the earth are
reputed as nothing: and he doeth according to

his will in the army of heaven, and among the inhabitants of the earth: and none can stay his hand, or say unto him, What doest thou?

At the same time my reason returned unto me; and for the glory of my kingdom, mine honour and brightness returned unto me; and my counsellors and my lords sought unto me; and I was established in my kingdom, and excellent majesty was added unto me.

Now I Nebuchadnezzar praise and extol and honour the King of heaven, all whose works are truth, and his ways judgment: and those that walk in pride he is able to abase.

It took some special, handcrafted torments to happen to the king before he recognized and acknowledged God for who He is. Only then could King Nebuchadnezzar regard himself and all people of the earth as nothing. Because of his trial, he could say with great fanaticism that God is God and that He can do whatever satisfies Himself to whomever He pleases. You, too, must realize there is nothing that can hold God's hand, and there is no right or authority to question whatever God does.

It is only when true revelation of God takes place that a hedge is positioned around those who have surrendered everything to God—then you realize you are nothing without Him. This then regulates, fixes, or adjusts the time or degree of permission the enemy has toward you. He can only go so far now that you are protected under the blood of Jesus. The blood of Jesus is against Satan, and there is no weapon formed against God's people that will prosper. Anyone who rises up against God's people in judgment is going to be condemned. The blood of Jesus protects us from all manners of evil and shields us against every diabolical, wicked, and cruel attack and assignment of the enemy.

As believers of Christ and His redemptive blood, we will not be so quick to see someone else's "stuff" if it continually reminds ourselves of the shortcomings we have overcome. The memory should automatically reflect your own heap of sin covered under the blood of Jesus. The next time you think about discussing, confronting, or engaging in useless chatter about someone else's mess, put your own face there, and then see what comes out.

We must continue to know that we have safety under the blood of Jesus. The blood of Christ became atonement for mankind to be able to return to right fellowship with God the Father. This was the propitiation for our lost souls. Not only that, but there are great benefits to mankind through the suffering of Jesus's life. The blood has an expensive price tag on it that we will never be able to repay. This salvation did not come without great cost; this was the gift of God to all mankind, the gift of eternal life through the blood of Jesus Christ.

Just envision with me, if you will, Jesus's flesh-ripped body hanging on the cross of Calvary at the "place of the skull" called Golgotha. Before he reached this place there was a barbed crown of mockery placed on his head with a sign not far from him reading, "Jesus of Nazareth, King of the Jews." This so-called crown was made up of thorns and thistles—prickly, sharp, rigid plants that would pierce his very scalp and cranium. Let us take a look at some of the benefits of the blood of Jesus, which has been sacrificed for mankind. Just imagine with me the blood trickling down the face of Jesus as he hangs lifelessly on the cross. Imagine each individual droplet of blood as it pours off the body of Jesus with a name inside each droplet. The blood bubble encases a message inside it. Just imagine, in our tiny, definably limited minds, the picture of one of many droplets pouring down Jesus's right check with the name "migraine" written inside it. Then look at another drop rolling down His forehead with the words "mental illness" written in it. Just as Jesus begins to hang His head and give up His life, there is another droplet that lands on His very eyelash that reads "blindness." A huge drop has entered the ear of Jesus, reading "death" to unstop death's ears. All these droplets have significance. They were shed with the purpose of the mind of God. God had your perfect health in mind when He put himself inside of himself, in the form of his son, that he would be given and broken for us. So whatever ailments are hindering you, be mindful of Isaiah 53:4–5.

*Surely he hath borne our griefs, and carried
our sorrows: yet we did esteem him stricken,
smitten of God, and afflicted.*

*But he was wounded for our transgressions;
he was bruised for our iniquities: the chastisement
of our peace was upon him; and with his stripes
we are healed.*

Jesus's suffering was not in vain. His wounds were not because he enjoyed being persecuted, whipped, and beaten. They were for every ungodly act we played out in our lives willingly, but Jesus's action didn't end there. He was wounded for our transgressions. He was bruised even for our iniquities. This is when you had no intentions of doing the right thing. This is when you intend in your heart to do evil and have stepped out of the very nature of God's creation to commit a sinful act. This was the perversion of your heart as a sinful man. But the blood of Jesus was shed for *all* that stuff. Jesus's bruises and the surface injuries to his flesh, along with contusions, were the result of our iniquities. Jesus took the lashes and whips so you and I could enjoy abundant life and not a life of sinful acts and shameful ways. He took it so we could turn away from the enjoyment of the sin nature that leads to a life of destruction.

So if Jesus did it for you and me, the same blood applies to others who desire a better life in Christ, with all their "stuff" covered under the blood. Let us remember to keep the blood of Jesus fresh, pure, and vigorous in our day-to-day lives. Do not allow the memories of what the blood of Jesus Christ has done for you to become stale, sour, decayed, or dried up. Remember, there is safety in the name of Jesus. Allow the word of God, the name of Jesus, and the blood of Jesus to remain the focus of your being, purpose, and existence.

Let us pray:

*Holy Father, in the name of Jesus, I thank you for the
precious blood of Jesus Christ, my Lord and Savior.
Father, I bless you for sending your only begotten*

son so that I might have life because of your love for your creation. Father, I ask you to forgive me of my sins of omission, when I omitted to do that which you instructed me to do it. You told me in your word to love one another and by this shall all men know that ye are my disciples, if ye have love one to another (John 13:35). Help me know that the power of the blood was not just for some but for all who would accept you as Lord. I accept you as Lord and I thank you for the blood cleansing me from all unrighteousness for your name's sake. Create in me a clean heart, Lord, and renew the right spirit within me. Cleanse my thoughts from past failures, habits, mistakes, and faults, and allow a refreshing to pour into my spirit that only the blood of Jesus can fill. Holy Father, I thank you for washing my sins away and making me as white as snow through the precious blood of Jesus. Have your way in my life, and use me for your glory and your honor that I will forever praise your name. In the matchless, wonderful name of Jesus I do pray.

Amen.

Poem

"THERE IS SAFETY UNDER THE BLOOD"

You've been under fire,
You've been under a fist,
You've been under the bed,
Trying to escape from "high risk"—
Toxic and abnormal,
You tolerated for so long,
You hope and pray one day he'd be gone.
The hand of a man is not what will keep you—
It is the blood of Jesus whose love is sincere and true
He won't hit you or beat you,
He's too much of a man; He wants your whole heart
And that He will not demand.
He's gentle and kind and His blood is so pure,
It cleanses and purifies through all you have endured.
So allow yourself to come up under
The relationship no man can put asunder—
There is safety under the Blood of
JESUS

NOTES

_____

_____

_____

_____

_____

_____

_____

_____

_____

_____

_____

_____

_____

_____

_____

_____

_____

_____

_____

_____

_____

_____

_____

CHAPTER SIX

THE PRAYING WOMAN IN YOU

Confess your faults one to another, and pray one
for another, that ye may be healed.
The effectual fervent prayer of a righteous
man availeth much.
James 5:16

It is not always easy to pray when situations arise in your life. In these times it seems there is no way out and prayer is the farthest duty from your mind. Sometimes concentrating with extreme diligence on how to come out of the situation becomes the real focus. When we finally discover where we are, the questions we tend to pose are these: "How did I get here?" "What have I done to put myself in this mess?" At this time, it seems as if our primary focus is on trying to untangle the web we wove to get ourselves in the mess in the first place. We go back in our thoughts and begin to examine our steps, trying to figure out at which point we made the wrong turn. Was I walking when I should have been absolutely still? Did I walk at a slow pace when I should have run like an athlete? Did I take one hour too long to obey the command that I heard in my spirit?

Whether the trial was of our own doing or was allowed by God to temper us, we must remember to use the right language while going through it.

We tend to add adjectives to our situations while we are in them. What do I mean by an adjective? An adjective is a word not standing by itself: it is dependent on another word to make a clear, valid, and concise point. An adjective is of, or relating to or requiring. When we enter a situation, we may enhance it by using adjectives while going through it. This only makes for a longer process.

For instance, "This is an outrageous request; I will not do it that way." Now, not only are you focused on how unpleasant or harmful or even highly offensive the request may have been to you, but you make it that much more difficult to complete. Because now you murmur, you complain, and it takes longer to get it done. Unbeknownst to you, the end result of the command was foretold to the commander to work out far better than you could have imagined.

What is really happening when we protest and object the instruction is that we are saying, "This storm is too big for me, and I do not want the blessing at the end of this trial."

The trial has been allowed to prove who and what we are made of. So stop crying over the trials and tests that you are experiencing, because attached to each test is God's holy blessing. However, you have to continue to give God all the honor and glory due His name even while you are going through a trial. If God sees that he can trust you to praise Him no matter what is going on in your life, he will continue to fight on your behalf. There is a reason why God continually allows the angels charge over you, fighting on your behalf and warding off the schemes of the enemy. The pursuit that God has for his praise in the earth should be the same pursuit that we have to simply joy in Him. The more you go through and the more you can take, withstand, and endure, the greater the anointing that is going to be placed on your life. And the only way you can tolerate your storm is if your life is hid in Christ. If you have allowed God to be your refuge in a time of trouble, He will protect and shelter you through your storm.

But none of these storms happen just because you are this great, grand, magnificent person in whom God sees human strength. No. There is a place where God is trying to get you to show forth his glory here on earth. He wants to use your life and your tests to show others how abundantly gracious he is—that if you can only trust that God is making you right in the midst of a tempest that seems unending, He will use your life to show His greatness and glory on the earth.

After all, He is the one who has brought you out of darkness. He brought you out—bringing you into that marvelous light—to go and get those who are going through that very same thing God delivered you out of. God wants to show off his glory in you that others may see how capable He really is to deliver, set free, and use you for his glory. We must remember that God is serious about his glory. God is jealous over his glory, and when you take on your own accomplishments as though they came from you, step aside because you are now standing in "vain glory."

So no matter what the situation is, pray to the Father, cry out to him in sincere repentance of heart. God said he will never leave us, nor will he forsake us (Hebrews 13:5–6). God says he will be with us always even until the ends of the world (Matthew 28:20). God told us that his thoughts toward us are good and not evil and will bring us to an expected end (Jeremiah 29:11). How can we forsake praying to the One who has such a covenant with us, even when we mess up? He is the One who knew we were going to mess up before we did. We must always thank Him for being such a merciful, forgiving, and loving God. God wants the glory out of our lives, and he wants to show those who are in the world that he is God, and besides him there is no other. And believe it or not, God wants to do that through all who are willing to take the time to pray to the Father, the Creator, and ask Him the question, "What will you do with this life you created in me?" I guarantee if you ask and believe that God hears your prayers, your answer will come.

Even when Jesus found himself in tough situations, what did he do? We say the words all too often without considering the question with earnestness: "What would Jesus do?—WWJD?" We sometimes use this saying as a cliché, but it is more than a few simple words to recite. It points you to the manual to guide you through tough circumstances. Look at your situation closely, then get the manual of life (the Bible), find the example of what you are going through in the word of God, and then act upon the instructions for a victorious outcome.

When Jesus fed the multitudes with the two fish and five loaves, the question was asked "what is in the midst to eat?" Matthew 14:15–17 states,

And when it was evening, his disciples came to him, saying, This is a desert place, and the time is now past; send the multitude away, that they may go into the villages, and buy themselves victuals.

But Jesus said unto them, they need not depart; give ye them to eat.

And they say unto him, we have here but five loaves, and two fishes.

Jesus was fully aware of their geographical location, the desert. Jesus was also privy to the amount of time the multitude had followed him. At all cost, try to avoid going to Jesus and telling him things that he already knows to produce your expected outcome. But even after the disciples complied, they were concerned about the quantity of food among them. The word *but* was emphasized when the disciples answered the question Jesus asked. The word *but* here implies "only." The disciples were actually saying, "We only have two 'little' fish and five 'small,' wafers, which is equivalent to a little boy's lunch." They saw the circumstances and began to complain. How many times have you looked at your circumstance and avoided seeing the big picture? Here we have a great number of hungry, tired, and exhausted believers—followers and lovers of Jesus—who are fatigued and maybe starving by now, and all we have is one lad's lunch. But instead of focusing on the size and quantity of the lunch, the focus should have been on who the disciples had in their midst and the miracle about to take place. We must know beyond a shadow of a doubt that if Jesus commands anything, He is definitely the one who has a plan to back it up.

Jesus took what they thought was not enough—the two little fishes and five small loaves—and blessed the multitude. The blessing did not solely manifest because the food was placed in Jesus's hand.

The miracle happened because He prayed to the Father. Jesus took what appeared not to be enough for the people, acknowledged the Father for that which was provided (He prayed), broke it, and only then did it become enough for the thousands of hungry, faithful followers.

Even in our brokenness, God is continually using that situation so that somewhere it will be a blessing for thousands…or maybe for just one. The situation that you just came out of is going to bless the multitude of others traveling through the same pathway, providing you are obedient in allowing the Lord to use you and your situation for *HIS* glory. Never look at what you are going through with adjectives attached to your words, such as "this is too *heavy*"; "I cannot handle this *gigantic* load"; "it feels like I am bearing an *enormous* cross." Keep your mouth off the test, and go through it and ask the Lord, "What am I to learn through this test? How can this test make me better than I was before I started this trial? What needs to come out of me to make me more like you as I go through this valley experience?"

Always look for God in what you are going through. Do not focus solely on the circumstance; look at yourself on the other side of your trial, finished, done, and complete. Do you see yourself being defeated by your trial with no way of escape? Or do you see the light at the end of the tunnel and know that you are going to come out of it a winner? 1 Corinthians 10:13 states,

There hath no temptation taken you but such as is common to man: but God is faithful, who will not suffer you to be tempted above that ye are able; but will with the temptation also make a way to escape, that ye may be able to bear it.

So whether you are provoked or strategically placed in a frustrating position, you must always make reference to the creator of all things, Our Father.

How do you see yourself at the end of your trial? You must rejoice in it. As you continually rejoice in your trial even though you do not feel like it, God is saying, "I can still trust her even through a trial to relentlessly give me the praise." See yourself victorious while you are in the middle of it.

However, getting to that point takes a consistent, fervent, effectual, diligent prayer lifestyle. We must acknowledge God in everything we go through, in everything we do, and in all our ways. Prayer is truly the only way to navigate through life's circumstances while continuing to believe that the situation will pass away or become better as long as we keep our trust in God.

We must realize how blessed we are, especially as women of God. Once we know and believe this for our own personal lives, we will then begin to walk in the authority and power given to us to trample over the enemy's schemes, plans, and evil devices. The Lord God Almighty is very mindful of us as women of God; once Eve responded to the question God asked her in regard to what she had done in the midst of the garden, immediately took action. Because Eve was beguiled, tricked, fooled by the serpent, God said in Genesis 3:13–16,

And the LORD God said unto the woman, what is this that thou hast done? And the woman said, the serpent beguiled me, and I did eat.

And the LORD God said unto the serpent, Because thou hast done this, thou art cursed above all cattle, and above every beast of the field; upon thy belly shalt thou go, and dust shalt thou eat all the days of thy life:

And I will put enmity between thee and the woman, and between thy seed and her seed; it shall bruise thy head, and thou shalt bruise his heel.

Then God went straight to the serpent to evoke a punishment on him for the trickery, deceit, and enticing he had used on Eve to get her to eat of the tree of the knowledge of good and evil (Genesis 2:17). The Lord God said to the serpent, "Because you hoodwinked and double-crossed the woman I ordained and blessed for Adam, I am going to pronounce a curse on you that puts you lower than all cattle and lower than every beast of the field." He told the serpent that he would have to maneuver through life on his belly and eat dust for the rest of his days.

It is not excessive that God went to this extent to pronounce judgment onto the serpent for his devious actions.

God emphasized His plan for the woman to have an aggressive and hostile attitude toward the devil. He said, "I will put enmity between thee and the devil." Enmity is a mutual hatred. God went straight to the serpent to reprimand him for the deceitfulness he enticed Eve with. Women, we have been given an irreconcilable, mutual hatred toward the devil that makes it impossible to be friendly or to be in harmony with him. The irreconcilable hatred that women have toward the devil is a weapon. With permission from God, one of the authorities of the woman is to pray against the evil forces of darkness that are set up against our husbands, our families, and our churches with great recompense. Compensation comes when the prayers of the woman tear down kingdoms and the evil forces of darkness. Because Satan caused women to have much grief and suffering in childbirth, God allowed women to have a great hatred toward Satan himself. The Lord has allowed us to have a holy hatred of all forms of evil.

What was God's intended purpose and desire for the woman before she ate the fruit and gave it to her husband? Genesis 2:20 states,

And Adam gave names to all cattle, and to the fowl of the air and to every beast of the field; but for Adam there was not found an help meet for him.

The Lord God is very mindful of the woman. He had a plan for the woman to be a help to her husband and not to become a hindrance. He wanted the woman to encourage her husband in the work God himself orchestrated for the man's life. The dominion, authority, and power given to Adam were never meant to be distorted. However, because Eve was beguiled, she stepped out of what sustained her (Adam) and listened to the sound of another voice. That is when death stepped in. This was the death of innocence. Satan, the master of deception and the progenitor of disobedience, wanted some more company, so he tricked Eve. Adam was very correct when he responded to the Lord that "the woman you gave me" was the reason he did it. Genesis 3:12 states,

And the man said, The woman whom thou gavest
to be with me, she gave me of the tree, and I did eat.

Yes, Eve was given to Adam; she was his gift from God. Women must know the correct voice to listen to. If women concentrate on hearing God and knowing His voice, women will no longer be confused by the enemy. The distinction of who is talking can be made unclouded by continuing to have relevant communication, supplication, and thanksgiving to the Lord. When women, especially, begin to meditate on all the Lord has done for them, how the Lord brought them out of situations and circumstances, it becomes that much easier to trust and rely on God's way and plan to move them to the next level. However, to maintain an uninterrupted, listening ear to the voice of God takes continual conversation, continual thanksgiving, continual praise and adoration to the Lord. These are all relative to your everyday walk with God. As you meditate on the things of God, your petitions and appeals will be heard by the Lord.

Knowing the voice of God is extremely important. If you are unsure if the Lord approves a matter or has an unfavorable opinion of a matter, you may resort to the possibility of accepting the voice of man. The word of God states in Jeremiah 17:5,

Thus saith the Lord; Cursed be the man that
trusteth in man, and maketh flesh his arm, and
whose heart departeth from the Lord.

God does not want His people to depend on the strength of another bodily creature He created. According to the book of Jeremiah chapter 17, refers to the sin and rebellion of the people who refused to show reverence to the Lord in their lives. Mankind has to always hold the Lord Jesus Christ in the highest regard. The awe and reverence of God must always remain in everything you do. The word of God also states in Psalms 118:8,

It is better to trust in the Lord than to put
confidence in man.

We must know the Lord for ourselves and know the sureness and confidence of the life we desire in Christ can only come from God. Prayer is a pertinent instrument for maturation and growth in our continuing path to eternal life. Prayer is a sharpened weapon in the arsenal of protective covering the Lord has granted to you for continual access to Him. When you pray, God is more than able to help you at your point of need. Jesus as the High Priest can sympathize and identify with your every weakness. It is vitally essential to retain a constant attitude of prayer and communication to God.

Prayer is not a cure-all to problems all by itself. We have a responsibility according to 2 Chronicles 7:14 if we are to be considered God's people:

> *If my people, which are called by my name,*
> *shall humble themselves, and pray, and seek*
> *my face, and turn from their wicked ways;*
> *then will I hear from heaven, and will forgive*
> *their sins, and will heal their land.*

Faith, trust, and confidence in God are active participating factors that initiate prayer. But getting to a consistent, fervent, and diligent prayer lifestyle does not happen overnight. As I stated in chapter 2, "Accept the Gift," if there is anything you enjoy, love, or appreciate, you spend time in it, around it, and with it. Every relationship has to be cultivated, developed, and nurtured. This allows you the time to get to know and recognize a person, place, or thing.

It is the same way with God. We have to take the time to get to know God's character, His voice, His silence, and His attitude. These attributes become more and more recognizable when valuable, meaningful time is spent with Him. With quality time spent in prayer, you will begin to distinguish the voice of God. You then will be able to differentiate between God's voice, your voice, and the voice of the devil.

However, we cannot come to God as though he is a relationship gone wrong or a buddy from down the road. We must recognize God as creator and sustainer of the universe. We must revere who God is and count him worthy of all honor, all glory, and all respect above all things established for mankind. Our very own conscience gives witness to the existence of God. The very breath we use to speak to God belongs to God. If God did not allow us to have the breath in our bodies, there would be no communication with Him.

In nothingness, God took and made something out of it. God wrapped himself in spirit and placed His spirit inside of flesh. The sole purpose of this act was for Him to continually be glorified. We must grasp and apprehend the fact that everything God does; He does for the praise of His glory. Isaiah 43:7 and 11 states,

Even every one that is called by my name:
for I have created him for my glory, I have
formed him; yea, I have made him.

I, even I, am the Lord; and beside me
there is no Saviour.

There is no other like the Lord. He is King of all Kings and Lord of all Lords. So how do you present yourself to God in prayer so that he is glorified? We first present ourselves to God with praise. Psalms 150:6 states,

Let everything that hath breath praise the Lord.
Praise ye the Lord.

God wants us to continually present ourselves in praise to him in devotion and worship. He never wants us to stop, and He always wants us to praise Him. Whenever we praise God, we are expressing a favorable finding to Him. We are exalting God for who he is and not just for what he can do or has already done. We can praise him for the birds that sing lullabies to us early in the morning. We can praise God for just being able to recognize Him as the Supreme Presence, the Highest Existence that he is, because some people, even today, still do not get it. When we praise God, we are saying, "God, I am praising you especially for the beauty of your perfection." Your praise should never be predicated on what God has given you or whom He has given you, but simply because *He is.* Let your praise always linger and remain in all that you do, especially entering into prayer.

Thanksgiving is another command we are to obey concerning how we present ourselves back to him through prayer. We must always keep an attitude of gratitude. Thanksgiving can be a prayer expressing nothing but gratitude toward the love of God. I often express to people how important it is to keep in the forefront of their minds what God has personally delivered them from…a constant reminder of why you praise God the way you do. This brings about verbal words of thanksgiving when going into prayer. By doing this you will always have a song of praise and thanksgiving on your heart and an expression of acknowledgment or celebration of God's divine goodness. Psalms 95:2 says,

> *Let us come before His presence with thanksgiving and make a joyful noise unto him with psalms.*

Your countenance should reflect great pleasure to abide, not looking for anything in return, but rather rendering a grateful attitude for who God is. How many times have we gone to God with our grocery list of "I Need, I Want, I Must Have"? How many honest bargain prayer people will say they went to God with their "Please do this for me and Lord I promise I will…" list? There is absolutely nothing wrong with asking God for your heart's desires. Matthew 7:7 states,

> *Ask, and it shall be given you; seek, and ye shall find; knock, and it shall be opened unto you:*
>
> *For every one that asketh receiveth; and he that seeketh findeth; and to him that knocketh it shall be opened.*

But oftentimes I believe the Lord want us to come before him with sincerity and express how grateful we already are without requesting anything in return. Praying with a thankful heart also tells God that we are aware of how mindful he is. God is so attentive and watchful of us that He will not grant us some of the request we petition of Him. God knows the outcome before the appeal is even made.

There are times you prayer could sound like this, "Lord, you know how badly I wanted that position, and I did not get it, but I trust that you know what is best for me, and I trust because you heard my prayer and you are covering me from an unseen danger, so Lord, thank you for not granting my petition." How many times do we look at unanswered prayers as a blessing from God instead of a curse or just a prayer that bounced off the ceiling? Let us try thanking God just for being so awesome and so powerful, so mighty and thoughtful and "all knowing" of us, to withhold that which is not good for us.

Psalms 100:1–4 reminds us why we should posture ourselves with praise and thanksgiving.

Make a joyful noise unto the Lord, all ye lands.

Serve the Lord with gladness: come
before his presence with singing.

Know ye that the Lord he is God: it is he that
hath made us, and not we ourselves;
we are his people, and the sheep of his pasture.

Enter into his gates with thanksgiving, and
into his courts with praise: be thankful
unto him, and bless his name.

There is no other way to enter into the presence of God except by way of reverence, respect and honor, praise and thanksgiving. Understand that we have been created to worship God. Not because all your bills are paid, your mortgage is not backed up, or the kids are on the honor roll in the finest schools on earth. These are all wonderful signs of good stewardship on your behalf and are worthy of a pat on the back. However, these are not the main, primary, or absolute reasons to be thankful and grateful enough to praise and thank God. The most important reason is simply because he is God.

Let us pray:

Most Holy Father, in the name of Jesus, I come to you because you are holy, you are my righteousness, you are awesome, and you are Sovereign. Lord, I thank you for creating me as a woman with an assignment. I thank and praise you for my sureness being in you. Thank you for being my rock, my refuge, and my God. In you and you only I will trust. I pray in the name of Jesus for a spirit of prayer over my life. Refresh and revive the praying woman in me. Awake in me the desire to spend intimate, special, relevant time with you. Lord, cast not your ears away from my presence, and receive me again into your loving arms through the words of my prayers, in the name of Jesus I pray.

Amen!

Poem

"THE PRAYING WOMAN IN YOU"

She was praying when you didn't even know,
Hoping you'd find the right way to go—
She saw your hurts and heard your cries,
She prayed and prayed that you would not die.
Now that you're still here it's your turn to pray
For those young ladies who have gone astray.
The path you once took, now leads them away;
They think it's their heart
So with their flesh they obey.
Pray for her now that God will save,
Give back to others as that one woman gave.

NOTES

_____

_____

_____

_____

_____

_____

_____

_____

_____

_____

_____

_____

_____

_____

_____

_____

_____

_____

_____

_____

_____

_____

_____

_____

_____

CHAPTER SEVEN

ℭℯ𝒩 𝒴𝒪𝒰 ℋℯ𝒩𝒟ℒℰ 𝒜𝒴 𝒩ℰ𝒲 𝒜ℯ𝒩?
CAN YOU HANDLE MY NEW MAN?

**Therefore if any man be in Christ,
he is a new creature: old things are passed
away; behold, all things are become new.
2 Corinthians 5**

As I begin this chapter it happens to be February 14, 2012—
Valentine's Day. The Westernized culture has adopted this as a
day of expression of love. The short version of how the day originated goes as follows. Some experts state that it originated from
St. Valentine, a Roman priest who was martyred for refusing to give
up Christianity and the right to marry a man and a woman who were
in love. St. Valentine served as a priest at the temple during the reign
of Emperor Claudius. Emperor Claudius's motives were solely to
encourage men to join his army, but they were unwilling to leave their
families. Before he suffered martyrdom, St. Valentine left a farewell
note for the jailer's daughter, who had become his friend, and signed it
"From Your Valentine." He died on February 14, 269 AD. In 496 .AD,
Pope Gelasius set aside February 14 to honor St. Valentine.

Perhaps a high school sweetheart or a crush from the guy in your
English class is a depiction of love. The serious, committed relationship that can possibly turn into marriage or a couple who believes
they are married to their "soul mate" for life are the result of love
happening somewhere. But the true act of unselfish and unveiling

love is the act of giving the only begotten Son on the cross of Calvary for remission of sin. This is the ultimate act of a *love* relationship. The familiar, famous passage of scripture St. John 3:16 says, "For God so loved the world, that he gave his only begotten Son, that whosoever believeth in him should not perish, but have everlasting life." This kind of love promises everlasting life. What a wonderful, incomparable gift that can only be given by the creator of the universe. By removing sin from the world, God disclosed how much he loves us and opened our eyes once again to how much he desires for us to have a love relationship with him. Love is an action word. It is something that you perform or do to express an emotion outwardly. God loved us so much that he gave up his only son that we could live an abundant life in Him. So, hands down, Jesus wins the award for best Valentine ever.

This is true only to those who have converted their lives and made Jesus their treasure. You will find that nothing can compare to the love he displayed and demonstrated for those he loves. Greater love has no man than this, that a man lay down his life for his friends (John 15:13). Jesus laid down his life for us. This outweighs the action of a crush, a companion, or even a spouse, who may have a desire to try to give you the world and his own life to express the love he has for you, but this is an act only Jesus could perform. And because Jesus did this for mankind—gave up his life so his friends could live—we have an obligation to realize and understand who we are here on earth. We have a binding agreement, a sense of duty, and a contract that is our guide to live by called the Holy Bible. The written word of God is our contract that records the examples of the acts of duties we are to perform and live accordingly.

2 Corinthians 5:17 it tells us how we are engrafted into a new form of life now that Jesus has laid down his life and we have accepted it as an act of love from the Father. It reads,

> *Therefore if any man be in Christ, he is a*
> *new creature; old thing are passed away;*
> *behold, all things are become new.*

A new creature denotes a freshness of the original formation or creation. The Greek word for creature is *ktisis*, meaning to create, form, or found. It also serves as an indication of something founded, such as a city—the colonization of a habitable place. A colony is a body of people living in a new territory but retaining ties with the parent state. Habitable means capable of being lived in, suitable for a living condition or habitation.

The word of God states that once you have accepted Jesus Christ as Lord into your heart and into your life, allowing His precious blood to cleanse you from all unrighteousness, all sin, and all iniquity, repenting and turning away from the stuff you used to do and allowing the Holy Spirit to abide within you *and* making Jesus your treasure, then you become a "new man" with the freshness of the original formation. The steps to becoming this "new man" should not be taken lightly. So there is no jumping past one step to get to the other. All steps are equally important to become who God intends you to be for His glory and honor. There are five crucial steps that must be fulfilled before we become joined or fasten as a functional, effective, authoritative, respected member of the body of Christ. I believe it is safe to say that all people want to be taken seriously in all they do (except if your profession is a clown). This is also true as a witness for Jesus Christ.

1. The first step is accepting Jesus Christ as Lord. A few definitions of the word *lord* in a general sense are as follows: one having power and authority over others, a man of rank or high position. Lord can also be a ruler by hereditary right or preeminence to whom service and obedience are due. Lord also means one who has achieved mastery or who exercises leadership or great power.

It is not enough just to accept Jesus Christ into your heart. You can accept the Lord Jesus Christ as your savior and go directly back to the place he wants you to be unchained from—the place of bondage and repression that is hindering you from telling anyone and everyone you can about Him. When you say yes to Jesus and accept him as your Lord and your Savior, you must also accept Jesus in your behavior, Jesus in your speech, Jesus in your mind, and Jesus in your sleep.

Jesus should be in your every thought. Everything you do, all that you say, what you think, and how you react should be patterned upon the way Jesus did it.

Once Jesus is accepted in every area of your life, you can now call Jesus "Lord." This says, "Lord, I give you power and authority over my life because you are one of high-ranking position." You are saying, "Lord, you rule and have preeminence to which service and obedience are due. Lord, you have achieved mastery and exercise leadership and great power by the example you demonstrate in the word of God. So here I am. Take my life and make sense of it for the glory of God."

The second step is allowing the blood of Jesus to do some cleaning up in your life.

2. Before allowing the blood to cleanse you from unrigh-teousness, you must believe the blood of Jesus that was shed for the remission (to pardon, or to release from the guilt or penalty) of sin and has the power to cleanse everything in your life unpleasing to God. In Hebrews 9:13–14 it says this,

> *For if the blood of bulls and of goats and*
> *the ashes of a heifer sprinkling the "unclean",*
> *sanctifies (to set apart to a sacred purpose)*
> *to the purifying of the flesh;*
>
> *How much more shall the blood of Christ,*
> *who through the eternal Spirit offered himself*
> *without spot to God, purge your conscience*
> *from dead works to serve the living God?*

The blood of Jesus has the power to flush out and remove every evil thought, erase every wicked deed, and massage the stoned heart into a functioning tool for God's purpose and for God's use. We must literally see those guilty verdicts (we deserved) pinned to the blood-stained body of Jesus on the cross of Calvary. Every sin and all iniquity (wickedness and injustice), the blood covers. We must let it go and allow our sins to be concealed under the blood of Jesus. I command you in the name of Jesus to get the vision and let it go.

Step number three is to repent and not return to those thing(s) that keep you from honoring God.

3. To repent means to turn upon or toward; a change of place or condition; to exercise the mind, think, or comprehend. Repentance is a sincere turning away from a condition, a genuine turning away from a certain way of thinking and turning your every motive toward God and His purpose for your life. Repentance is having a sensitivity of regret or sorrow enough not to do it again. The regret or sorrow is so dreadful that you will never want to suffer or experience the feeling ever again. That is how true heartfelt repentance compels you to react. If there is no deep, bona fide sorrow inside you for the act committed, it is not repentance. If you do not undergo a sense of unworthiness, degradation, and shame for what you did enough to turn away from it, knowing you are estranged from God, it is not true repentance. Repentance will not be lip service only, but an appropriate and immediate spiraling away from that which keeps you separated from God. That is repentance.

Step number four is inviting the Holy Spirit to abide in you.

4. When the Holy Spirit is invited in, you are saying, "Holy Spirit, you are welcome in this place; Holy Spirit, you are welcome in my life; and Holy Spirit, you are welcome into my heart." Acts 1:8 states,

*But ye shall receive power after that
the Holy Ghost is come upon you: and ye
shall be witnesses unto me both in Jerusalem
and in all Judea and in Samaria and unto the
uttermost part of the earth.*

Let us be certain that we understand the Holy Spirit cannot rest, reside, abide, or live in a place already occupied with its own agenda. If sin of any kind is in your house, figuratively or naturally, He will not come in. For example, women, if you are living with a man whom you are not married to, but you both decided to save money before the wedding and are sleeping in the same bed, trust me, temptation is there and more than likely having its way—the Holy Spirit is not coming in there. There is already an agenda going on, and there is no place for Him.

The Holy Spirit is a loquacious, long-winded gentleman. He is always speaking. He will not force himself on anyone. The Holy Spirit wants to live in a place where He has total control to lead you and guide into the truth. John 16:13 reads,

Howbeit when he, the Spirit of truth is come,
he will guide you into all truth: for he shall not
speak of himself: but whatsoever he shall hear,
that shall he speak and he will show
you things to come.

1 Corinthians 6:19 states,

What? Know ye not that your body is the
temple of the Holy Ghost which is in you,
which ye have of God and ye are not your own.

Once you realize that God wants you to become enamored with Him and wants you to be covered every step of the way through your journey of salvation, then you will do whatever is needed to allow the Holy Spirit to abide within you.

Step five is to make Jesus your treasure.

5. What exactly is a treasure? What do you do with something you treasure? Why is your treasure so valuable to you? What gives your treasure its worth?

A treasure is something of significant value and worth to you. It has major importance to you. It is esteemed as rare or precious.

The book of Matthew 6:21 shares,

For where your treasure is, there will your heart be also.

The Greek word for heart here is *kardia,* which means the seat and center of human life. Our heart and mind hold the seat of our desires, feelings, affections, passions, and impulses. How much of our heart seizes, occupies, or grabs hold of Jesus being our treasure, the jewel of our sanctified life? Is Jesus in the center of your human life? Is Jesus the center of your joy? If you are attempting to live life without Jesus Christ, you merely exist. God does not want you to simply exist; He wants to use your life for His glory and His honor.

At this time, if you have accepted Jesus as Lord, the blood has cleansed, repentance has taken place, the Holy Spirit is welcomed, and Jesus has been made a most trusted treasure, now you are in a suitable position for the Lord to habitat with you by way of the Holy Spirit. Now the Holy Spirit does not have to contend for space in your life. Now God can talk to you and abide with you because He parents everything about you. God is the material or source from which we are derived. He can now tabernacle with you, dwell within you, now that you have allowed yourself to come to the end of yourself.

2 Corinthians 5:17–18 says,

Therefore if any man be in Christ, he is a
new creature: old things are passed away;
behold, all things are become new.

And all things are of God, who hath
reconciled us to himself by Jesus Christ, and
hath given to us the ministry of reconciliation;

It says that old things have passed away, and look, behold, all things have become new. When all things become new, the word is saying that we should now have a new way of talking, a new way of walking, a new way of living, and even a new way of thinking.

You remember what you used to be, right? The thoughts, the dreams, the works, and the actions of an "enemy-controlled" mind that ruled, governed, and dictated your every move. Were you not ecstatic and delighted to know your slate was wiped clean? Were you not extremely happy to know the accusations you should have been convicted of in the sight of God were cancelled? The ballot was now blank. It was clear the night you should have gone into a coma because of the bountiful quantity of drugs introduced and activated into your bloodstream. The slate was erased of the abortion you had because of the fear of what people would say because you were unwed. You remember. The night at the club when your drink tasted kind of funny and the next thing you knew you were at your apartment and did not remember how you got there or who just left. But God's mercy and grace keep you from all dangers. He kept you from dangers seen and unseen. You did not see the ministering angels surrounding the vehicle and the driver who got you home safely. I am sure, if we are honest with ourselves, we all have a story that points us back to the only explanation for us not being consumed while in our sin—the grace and mercy of God.

I mention these scenarios because if we can forever remember our own sins, we will have no time to convict anyone else of theirs. So if all of your stuff is under the blood of Jesus, why can't you leave others' there, too? There is enough room under the blood for all of their garbage, too. Can you *not* see the new man emerging? Can you *not* see the effort and steps being taken to get their lives right? You have to meet people right where they are and not bash them while they are trying to get it together. Why is it that other people's ways do not look different to some people? They just refuse to see the change in another person's life. Or they just flat out overlook the miraculous transformation that is taking place in another person's life right before their very eyes. If you are struggling with this, could it be their new man is blinding to you because you may be struggling with some issues yourself? Remember, there was someone there to encourage you when difficulties came to your front door. How soon we forget our struggles. No, we do not have to live in them, but for God's sake, do not forget them to the point you act as though you have never been delivered from refuse and filth of some sort. Keep in mind the struggles you have overcome to become who you are today, remembering it was only by the grace of God in your life. He has made you into a new man, a new creation.

The primary focus now is to concentrate on what is before you. This is what Apostle Paul meant by stating we should press toward the mark for the prize of the high calling of God in Christ Jesus (Philippians 3:14). To press means to push on with force, to move and to bear heavily. And this is done with a goal in mind. The goal is the high calling of God. What is this high calling? In the Greek the word *high* here is *ano*, which means upward or on the top, above or high up. Apostle Paul emphasized the importance of forgetting those things that happened in the past so our focus can be shifted to getting to heaven some day and experiencing eternal life. That is the high prize, the above calling, and the upward goal.

True believers of God's deliverance and power by the remissions of our sins through Jesus Christ our Lord must be mindful of the new converts who come into our church houses with residue they are desperately trying to escape. Just remember what God snatched you out of. Once you have kept that in mind, not only will these new converts receive you, but they will also detect a heartfelt, sincere cry on their behalf. This will show them the true love of Christ. And it also will make them say, "Wow, they are really doing the Bible here at this church! She is praying for me as if she was the one going through this thing." How powerful if that new believer saw scripture being fulfilled through an actual believer's demonstration right before her very eyes. She will say, "What she has done is Matthew 19:19…she loves me as herself. She prayed for me the way I would suppose she prays for herself, with vigor, enthusiasm, and energy."

Thou shalt love thy neighbour as thyself.

Matthew 19:19b, the word *love* means to love in a social or a moral sense. It is a shared or communal sense of concern for the well-being of another. This love expresses a good and proper response of a decent and honest manner. When we love another as ourselves, we show forth the love of Christ within us. The word *neighbor* here is relating to someone close by or near, a fellow or friend. This is the way we should see our brothers and sisters in the Lord at all times, not as our enemies.

We should all see ourselves on the same playing fields, but in different positions, as in 1 Corinthians 12:19–21:

*And if they were all one member,
where were the body?*

*But now are they many members, yet but
one body. And the eye cannot say unto the hand,
I have no need of thee: nor again the
head to the feet, I have no need of you.*

As the body of Christ, we all have need of one another. It is time to work your "*new man*" for the edifying of the body, to perfecting the saints until we all come into the unity of the faith. This is not the time to have envy toward your brother or sister (as if there is any time that you should). This is the time to embrace the talents, gifts, and abilities that God gave them for His honor and glory. They are only to edify the body so all can become mature.

Consider the fact of your neighbor being a new creature with a freshness of the original formation or creation. There is no time to "hate" on your sister or try to hit on your brother; we have a work to do for the Kingdom of God to the glory and honor due His name, together.

As the word states in 1 Peter 2:9,

*But ye are a chosen generation,
a royal priesthood, a holy nation,
a peculiar people that ye should show
forth the praises of him who haveth called
you out of darkness into his marvelous light.*

So the question to ask is this: Can I tolerate, embrace and receive the "new man" of my fellow brothers and sisters in Christ? Am I going to criticize, antagonize, and aggravate the work the Lord has done in their lives? Or will I capture the illumination of God's glory because I too was once without hope, but now I know it is only the workings of God in my life and in theirs as well?

Let us pray:

Glorious Father, in the name of Jesus,

I thank you for creating in me a new heart, Lord, and Lord, I thank you for renewing the right spirit within me. The right spirit is your Holy Spirit. I thank you for the newness of life inside of me that gives me another opportunity to live as you have designed for me initially. Lord, I thank you for giving me another chance to glorify you here on earth. Thank you for being mindful of me when I did not even mind my own self. Have mercy upon me, and allow your new mercies to abide with me always. Lord, I love you because you are perfect in all your ways. I thank you that your ways are not my ways and your thoughts are not my thoughts. I pray that you will continue to allow the Holy Spirit to lead me into all truths. And Lord, forgive me for not treating others as myself, and forgive me for esteeming myself higher than I should have. Lord, you have no respect of persons, and I should not have any either. Forgive me of my sin, and wash me afresh in the precious blood of the Lamb—Jesus, my Lord. Thank you, Lord. In Jesus's name I do pray.

Amen!

Poem

"CAN YOU HANDLE MY NEW MAN?"

Who is this new man they keep talking about?
Is he six figures tall or intellectually stout?
"Who is He?" Who is He? ...
I want to SEE.
Girl, how can I get the hookup for you and for me?
"Who is this new man you say I can't handle?"
Girl, your hands can't even touch HIS sandal.
So settle down, settle down, you get too excited
About a flesh man who's not even ignited.
The new man is Christ.
He lives within me—
He is the only WAY to True victory.

NOTES

_____

_____

_____

_____

_____

_____

_____

_____

_____

_____

_____

_____

_____

_____

_____

_____

_____

_____

_____

_____

_____

_____

_____

CHAPTER EIGHT

HE LOVES ME, HE LOVES ME RIGHT!

We love Him because He first loved us.
1 John 4:19

To recap on what has transpired thus far: Prayerfully you have forgiven yourself of past sins and behaviors displayed in your old life, as we learned in chapter 1. Hopefully in chapter 2 you have confessed to yourself and others the most embarrassing and unheard-of testaments of your life and accepted Jesus Christ as your God, your Lord and Savior. Now you may ask, "What is next?" Chapter 3 described the struggles and troubles you overcame after surrendering your life to Christ. Chapter 4 showed you how to conquer, defeat, and destroy the tactics of the enemy. But questions may remain: What is next for my life? How should I prepare for my new life in Christ? In chapter 5, you realized there is true safety when you are covered under the blood of Jesus Christ, and you have now found that there is power in the words of prayer, in chapter 6. You discovered that you possess an entire kingdom of authority, defense, protection, and kingship inside you. This fortified city of God is now living inside the "totally transformed, converted, delivered, sold-out for Jesus and Him alone" believer. This authority gives you the power to destroy the wiles of the enemy against your life and others by the authority and influence of prayer. Now with the authority, boldness, and confidence you have in Christ Jesus, you discover your new man is more powerful beyond measure, as we learned in chapter 7. You realize some cannot handle the light that now illuminates from the kingdom, the fortified city in you, because you have discontinued their employment. What do I mean by discontinued employment? As long as you continued to run to these people for validation, they were fine with you. Now that you have received strength from God, your true identity has been revealed to you, and you discovered that you too can talk to the Father on your own behalf and know He will answer you too, why will they have need of you? If at one point in time you relied on others to pray for you and asked questions that only God truly has the answer to, others no longer have the privilege to influence your decisions, your thought process, or your conflict resolutions. So your new man is now unaffected by them. They now have to find another party who has not yet come into the knowledge of the truth of who they are in the kingdom. In their eyes, there is no longer any use for you. But praise God for victory and liberty in Jesus.

This is when you take the opportunity to thank everyone (currently or previously) that is or has been in your life to provoke you to be where you are today. Be it a positive push or a negative, heart-wrenching shove, I encourage you to say thank you to those who have helped you get to this point in your life. (*Thank you all* greatly.) Continue to pray for them and love them regardless of how you were treated by them. God loved us when we were in our sin, when we did not want to come out of our sin, and even when we accepted him and failed him by sinning, God still loved us. God loves us 1,000 percent all the time. God loved us so much he showed his love toward us while we were yet sinners (Romans 5:8). 1 John 4:19 says it best,

We love Him because He first loved us.

We must remember that forgiveness is such a critical aspect of our walk with God. No matter the attack or accusation against you, forgiving someone else will free you from becoming bitter, angry, resentful, and/or ill.

Let us look at it from another angle. Imagine with me, if you will, we as human beings created as big bags of sand. Picture yourself walking along the shores of life, leaking along the way. The natural mind resorts to the thought of eventually becoming depleted, emptied, bare, and unfilled. But by God's design, we are to leak, pour out, and give away. The leakage is only because of the investment God has placed into our lives. These are assets intended to be shared among the millions of miles of the sanded seashores. The seashores represent broken people waiting for you to be the salt of the earth and the light of the world. Salt is an element that gives liveliness, sharp taste, or pungency. Light brings a brightness, luminosity, and radiance. Light brings explanation to objects unseen in the darkness. This is what the world is looking for in those who have had the privilege to accept Christ into their hearts in the pardon of our sins. The word of God states in Romans 8:22,

*For we know that the whole creation groaneth
and travaileth in pain together until now.*

God wants the revelation of His glory to come through those who will go all the way in Him. God is looking for himself in his creation.

Envision your bag as you are challenged to walk forward in life's journey but you continually look behind you in an attempt to go back and catch the grains of sand that are spilling out. What you are actually looking for is an apology from the childhood molester, an answer from the ex-spouse or former significant other, or the explanation of why it was your loved one who had to die in his or her adolescent years. Although you are looking for answers, you will never obtain the exact grains of sand that were emptied out. You are now collecting stuff that may resemble that which was poured out in the hope of an answer. These efforts are pointless. You may never get an apology or a response. Stop looking and stop expecting one—forgive them and move on. It is out of your control. Allow God to have power over your heart. Continue to bless God for allowing you to make it out in one piece, in your rightful mind, yearning for more of the Savior who has restored, mended, and recharged you.

It is God's design for you to empty yourself into the lives of others. God does not want you to hold on to past hurt, rejections, disappointments, and failures. He wants you to perfect the skill of excusing people who have treated you incorrectly. God wants to persistently and continually pour more of himself into you for His glory and honor. If you constantly strive to regain and collect that which is no longer relevant to where you are or where you are going (such as an apology or an I'm sorry), you will never get to spread your sand (salt and light) to the millions who are miles away waiting for you to get there. Focusing on how *they* did you wrong, why *they* did you wrong, if *they* will do you wrong again, if *they* are continuing to do other people wrong, exerts too much energy and expends too much time when you can be affecting the lives of others whom God has predestined for you to touch. You must let loose and give free rein to be the best person you can be. The closer you draw to your liberty, the more people will not want to be around you. So for those who cannot handle your new man, your newness of life, love them anyway and pray for them. When you do this, it is proof that you are a lover of God and you are fulfilling a command given you. 1 John 4:21 states,

And this commandment have we from him,
that he who loveth God love his brother also.

It does not say love your saved brother or your perfect brother. It just says to "love his brother also." Is it easy to do if they are treating you poorly? It absolutely is not! But is it necessary? It is highly crucial and extremely essential to love and forgive those offenders regardless of the transgression. Matthew chapter 5:43-44 shares with us how we should respond to our enemies.

Ye have heard that it hath been said,
Thou shalt love thy neighbour, and hate thine enemy.

But I say unto you, Love your enemies, bless
them that curse you, do good to them that

hate you, and pray for them which despitefully use you, and persecute you;

First let me define enemy. An enemy is a person who feels hatred for you. An enemy is one who fosters harmful designs against you or engages in antagonistic activities against you. Their actions speak as though you are their opponent, and you force them to go on the defensive, in protection and guard mode. For the most part, we should not have to shrink or minimize who we are as God's chosen vessels just to satisfy or appease those around us who may feel insecure when we show up on the scene. God intended for *all* his elect ones to shine as his glory on the earth. We sometimes fail to realize that we are on the same team. It has to be relentlessly understood that we are better together. Unity, agreement, and harmony are necessary to subdue the enemies' kingdom. The true enemy—the prince and power of the air, Satan, the ruler of darkness and wickedness in high places in this earth—is the primary perpetrator we should hate. Your sister or brother is *not* your true enemy. Even if he or she happens to be possessed, obsessed, crazed, or overcome by the influences of the adversary because of open portals and pathways of entry allowed by indulgence, ungodly pleasures, and sin, it is not "totally" his or her fault. Once these doorways are opened, access and authority are given for the demonic influences to control your thoughts, your mind, and your life unless you turn away from, run, flee, and avoid all instances of sin. Then you must denounce Satan and his forces as the principal authority in your life. That is why we should not give any evil spirit the opportunity to take possession of us through ungodly behavior, wicked ways of thinking, and perverted perceptions of life by denying the spirit of God to operate through us. So keep in mind that your sisters and brothers are not the true enemy here unless they have given way to the performances and activities directed by Satan himself. Therefore, love them with an unquestionable love whether they receive it from you or not. Give to others a love that is so wholesome and real that if you receive an unenthusiastic, apathetic, lukewarm response, it will not change your demonstration of authentic love. Love never fails. Love (charity) covers a multitude of sins.

1 Peter 4:8 states, "And above all things have fervent charity among yourselves; for charity shall cover the multitude of sins." Fervent is to be keen, avid and fanatical. Imagine being dedicated to loving others so outrageously and over abundantly that the action displayed by you becomes so overwhelming to the receivers that their response does not really matter because your part has been fulfilled.

Matthew 5:43–44 establishes the fact that love never fails. You cannot be defeated when you love. There is no failure or malfunction in love. We must do it according to the directions and guidelines the Lord has set before us as examples, loving others and doing it the right way—God's way.

Let us look at love. We all have the propensity, or a general inclination, to believe that we know what love is. In its most generic state, love is having tender affection or desire for somebody or something. Love is liking something very much or showing kindness to somebody. It represents a passionate attraction and desire with a very strong affection. Love is also depicted as a strong liking for or pleasure gained from someone. Love can be explained as a passionate feeling of romantic desires leading to sexual attraction and copulation.

God's loves demonstrated in the Bible are examples of how we should love, be loved, and love others. The word *Phileo* means friend. The Christians in the New Testament were commanded to love out of a common spiritual life for one another. They were to have mutual respect and taking the lead of each other. This meant having an unselfish concern for the well-being of your brother or sister. The mutual respect is when you pray for them in obedience and the prompting of the Holy Spirit. You may not have all the details surrounding why you are nudged to intercede at that moment, and you may never know the reason why. But if the Holy Spirit is leading you, then *Phileo* love says, "Yes, OK, I will pray for my brother or sister without question." Because of the love, the fraternal affection toward them, you just pray with no questions asked. The Spirit of God inside of you will direct and instruct you how to express your prayer and hit the target.

This love must be displayed without hypocrisy and double standards. This love must be unfeigned, not pretending or false. People can detect when your acts of love are true and sincere as well as distinguish fake and impure, distorted attempts to display love. The word *Phileo*—meaning friend—refers to one who is attached to another by respect or affection. A friend is one who supports or favors something. The *Phileo* love of a friend has your back when you have good ideas, good intentions, or simply need someone to listen to you. However, a true friend is also one who tells you the truth no matter how you may take it because of love. Friends will not reserve the right or "plead the fifth" to expose to you your behaviors, actions, or dealings if they perceive them to be headed in the wrong direction, not on the course of God. Because a person who is attached to you and respects and loves you will not allow you to fall in a ditch and just stand by to watch you drop to the bottom without any rescue attempt. Love does not look on as a friend enters into a danger zone and then turn away as though there is no destruction ahead. Love will not shut its eyes and mouth and say nothing or do nothing. 1 John 4:11 states, "Beloved, if God so loved us we ought also to love one another." Love proves to be an action, not just a word to throw around loosely. When you love something or someone, you do something about it.

The author of the book of Hebrews stresses in chapter 13 several recommendations of excellent duties to follow as pertaining to godliness. In verses 1 through 3 it states, "Let brotherly love continue. Be not forgetful to entertain strangers for thereby some have entertained angels unawares. Remembering them that are in bonds, as bound with them; and them which suffer adversity as being yourselves also in the body." When we see not only our brother or sister, but even a stranger, in a situation, we should have some compassion and empathy toward their position. A beggar or homeless person on the street has many dynamics that need to be sorted through to determine the root cause of their homelessness, but that does not stop us from being concerned or showing kindness toward them. On the other hand, brothers and sisters in Christ, please do not suggest that ministers, deacons, missionaries, elders, reverends, and pastors are trying to be "all up in your business"! They care less about your business but are more concerned about your soul, which is their business. How can you be helped, restored, or transformed if you do not allow someone else to genuinely care about what you are going through? Remember, verse 3 of Hebrews chapter 13 says, "to them that are in bonds as bound with them." The ordained ministerial staff is trained, is equipped, and wants to see you delivered only because of love. They see these brothers and sisters as being held captive by the sin they are in as prisoners in bonds. *Phileo* love will go the distance with you until your outcome is victorious—*only if you receive it and want out bad enough.* Some people are not tired of being tired or sick of being sick. The bottom has not dropped out; their backs are not against the wall yet because there are other options they can rely on to see them through. But when all else fails, there is a name above every drug dealer, hustler supplier, sugar daddy/momma, swindler, schemer, and extortionist. He is a gentleman and will not force himself on you or anyone else. His name is Jesus. Jesus is waiting with arms opened wide to receive those who may feel all hope is gone.

Phileo will be as a "breath of fresh air" after a long, hot, dry, and desolate journey where you could see no relief in sight. The action of *Phileo* will stand and fight with you in prayer and encourage you in the word and the things of God.

Brotherly love must be a fixed practice that is kept with us at all times, and we must never let it stop working. *Phileo* is never used as a command for men to "love" God, but rather as a "tender affection" toward one another.

There is another word most commonly used among those who have been raised and cultivated in church society, church background, church traditions, and the church environment as a whole. If you happen to be in that category, statements such as "I agape you" and "We must always show 'agape' love" may sound very memorable to you. This word, *agape* (pronounced ag-ah-pay), is an affectionate regard or benevolence (an act of kindness, a charitable gift and showing compassion) and goodwill. God is the author and the source of love. He is full of love and is *all* love. God's love does not require an approving reply from anyone or anything in order to continue to be God, who is love. God's love is unconditional—you cannot stop it from coming to you, nor do you have to do anything to be loved by God. Romans 5:8 states, "But God commendeth his love toward us, in that, while we were yet sinners, Christ died for us." The word *commendeth* in the Greek is *sunistao*, (pronounced soon-is-tah'o) meaning strengthened. Have you ever had to tighten up your love toward someone who trespassed against you? Have you ever had to strengthen your love toward someone who has done you wrong or caused an injury or offense against you? This is a difficult assignment to conquer. But God! But love! That is exactly what God did for mankind because of agape love. He loved us outrageously enough to identify His love by an action; He gave his only begotten Son, Jesus, as a ransom for you. God's love exceeded the limits that are unusual. Agape is not a word to be used frivolously or without due consideration. If we can barely overlook the usher not speaking to us on Sunday morning, how much more can we love an assassin who executed a close relative? Agape is the love shown to us in our undeserving, unworthy, contemptible state that only the all-loving, all-compassionate, Sovereign God can render. Agape is so absolute it would take another book to explain the sum.

In my challenge to illustrate how little we know about love and how forgiveness plays an important part in loving. Eros is the love that so many have twisted. Do we truly understand God's intended purpose for this type of love? Take one of the most popular US zip codes—90210. This is a district known to be well-to-do, prosperous, and fortunate, filled with to-be-envied folk. How many of you know that wealth will respond to a collection of concerns, but it cannot buy you love? No matter how much you wine and dine, purchase French-named automobiles and lavishly appointed homes, if you have no one to enjoy them with, their worth depreciates.

On multiple television programs today, you may see a couple out on a second date, having a casual dinner and conversation full of laughter and excitement. Then the very next scene is back at the woman's apartment in the bathroom with a hot, steaming shower door, behind which the duo are enjoying each other as though they were the last two on earth and there's no tomorrow. They met through a mutual friend at a going-away party, they were introduced, and now the second date led to her revealing herself to someone whose last name she may never know...or maybe she never even thought to ask if he had one. (Sidebar: Countless men today are not privy to the fact that they should have a legacy attached to their last name and not a heritage by the number of legs pried open that produced bastards (nevertheless that is another book.) These relations were built strictly on lustful desires and not love. The mutual moment in the shower was not a result of getting to know each other and having a great deal in common. It was not the result of a developed friendship and a shared interest, of similar goals and aspirations for life. It was not the desire to contribute to each other's lives because of similar likes and dislikes. This was nothing short of illicit eroticism, sensuality, and copulation. Where's the love? Where is the strong passionate desire and delight in one another's company without being intimate or having sex? Eros is an unbreakable love tie. This love is—to have a strong passionate desire and delight in. Love affords you to have a moderate (fair, restrained) feeling and emotion toward someone. With Eros there is a fondness, a liking, and a tender attachment to someone. This love is completely different from the type of love displayed by Mary and Martha toward their brother, Lazarus, in John 11. Lazarus died and was buried, and the deep sorrow and connectivity they shared with their brother was of a family love, a bond among siblings. This natural love and affection of a close relative is incomparable to the Eros love displayed between those desiring to become more.

Becoming friends first is extremely important. What comes to mind when you think of friends? You may say a friend is a hang-out buddy or someone you confide in, sharing the most intricate details of a significant circumstance going on in your life. Friends are those you can talk to about the things you wish you did not even know.

Imagine two childhood friends who grew up together, went to grade school and high school together, and did cheerleading and volleyball, and call themselves BFFs. I would be willing to guess that these two young ladies have collected more information and experience about each other than their own parents may know. Because they have spent an abundant amount of time together, they have now become recognizable, common, and well-known to one another. And this should be a focal point of relationships for those who have an internal longing to spend more than just one night with their suitor.

A suitor is a man who courts or woos a woman. A good number of people have never heard the word *woo* before, let alone exemplify or demonstrate the qualities of a person seeking the favor, fondness, or friendliness of another without taking him or her to bed first. If you are just friends first, his character should woo and entice you. The way he or she speaks and declares things should encourage you. The way he or she responds to others and carries him- or herself as a man or woman of standards should impress you. The person's values and morals should persuade you to want to get to know more about him or her. At this point you will know if you even like the person or not. It is OK to stop an attraction or magnetism at any point if you discover some qualities that make you uncomfortable. These are called "warning signs," "red flags," or "stop signs"—if you see them, don't go any further. Hypothetically speaking, if you are out on a movie date and your date becomes impatient and begins to raise his voice, then snatches you by the arm out of the car that is a sign. Do not ignore it, do not dismiss it, and do not act as though it did not take place just because your date is cute. Say, for instance, the two of you are at a restaurant having an amazing meal and enjoying one another when out of nowhere your date calls you a disgraceful name. When you decide to stand your ground in response to the negative comment, and your date begins to lean forward as though to intimidate you but then backs down, it was not your imagination. Those types of behaviors do not just happen, nor do they just happen to go away. These behavior types are real signs of something potentially damaging or detrimental that could take place in the future. It is OK to say, "All right, you know what, I'm out of here. I do not deserve to be treated like a back porch dog; you do not own me, nor am I morally obligated to stay in your presence."

Unfortunately, many potential couples have not bothered to find out if they even like each other as people, let alone as "friends." There must be a serious evaluation and thorough collection of data before others are allowed into intimate spaces. It should not be determined by, "Oh, I think he's cute," or "Did you check out his outfit and those shoes? That wallet was pretty thick, too." (Newsflash: People carrying their worth in their pockets or pocketbook have already displayed to you what they are really worth). There is no way you can ever know enough about anyone in two dates to be willing to render, deliver, or provide any type of act of love toward them. There may be a chance to become more than just acquaintances, but you must know the other party as a companion and not just by the currency in the pocket or his shoe size, ladies.

First of all, love does not hurt, nor does love seek its own advantage or take advantage of someone else. Love is kind, love is considerate, love understands. Love is sympathetic—love is compassionate and sensitive. If these attributes are absent, you may want to reevaluate whom you are giving your time and attention to. Any man or woman worth dating *should not* have a problem with waiting to have a more intimate relationship with you. It has to be made simple and perfectly clear that if the Christ in you is not respected as presenting your body unto Him as a living sacrifice, you will become compromised in what you stand for. It must become unmistakably, unequivocally clear that your date wants to get to know you as a person. Who are you? What are your dreams and aspirations? Most importantly, as a Christian woman who is saving herself for marriage, you must wait to seal the deal. Yes, I know this sounds like old-fashioned, down-on-the-farm, small-town-in-the-middle-of-nowhere advice, but if we model the examples of couples who have lived this way and find out what they did to remain married for more than thirty years to the same spouse, it may help us today in a society where anything goes. Many of these couples may come from close-knit communities, family-oriented backgrounds, and possibly two-parent homes. This is not to say a single parent could not raise a successful, well-mannered, intellectual child alone. The love given in a single-parent home could very well be equivalent to or even greater than in a two-parent home with both parents working and unable to show the act of real love toward their children.

It is understood that the world has a slightly different definition of friends. Some say, "We are friends with benefits." Well, what exactly does the reimbursement or repayment package consists of if you are friends with benefits? What are you willing to settle for just for the sake of saying you have a friend? Some may suggest, "We are just platonic friends, with added modifications and adjustments to the friendship." They do not engage in actual copulation but may conduct experiments. From the world's perspective, friends are those you call on when the special event at the company demands you have a trophy on your arm and without a trophy of a woman you will not be allowed. If there is not a date present with you who has the look the big bosses want to see, your promotion will not be considered. With this type of association, there is no sincerity, honesty, or heartfelt commitment toward each other. It is just an "outward" expression of friendship. These types of relationships suggest the thoughts, "I need you for my own personal reasons and nothing more." In other words,

"I need you only as a representation of what appears to be a great relationship, but I do not want a true relationship with you." Who does that and why? Do not devalue yourself. Who told you this is the best you can do? Some may fool themselves and say that at least they appear to have a date or someone who is interested in them. Or do you have a hidden agenda, too? Do not fool yourself, because if this is the way you think then there is something more serious going on than just you wanting to "look the part" and be accepted. This type of thinking suggests that you are settling and cheapening your self-worth. No one deserves to be used or looked upon as a beautiful casing with no contents inside. Some people believe that having an intellectual mind is more attractive than beauty, and if you happen to have both, count it all joy.

Nevertheless, Christians desiring to establish friendships first in a relationship should make perfectly clear each individual's definition of a friend. This should be totally unidentifiable as the world's view of a friend. As a Christian, one of the *primary* focal points should be if Jesus Christ is your Lord and Savior. For starters, it is important to know if you both are on the same wavelength. It is perfectly OK to ask your "friend candidate" questions about his relationship with the Lord. If he responds by saying, "This is not a topic up for discussion" or "Why do we have to talk about that?" then you have the right to question the validity of his answer to the question of whether Jesus Christ is his Lord and Savior. Please do not misunderstand—conversations will not always be about the things of God; however, if it starts off as an "offense" and is an uncomfortable conversation for one person, this is *not* a good sign. Honesty is crucial from the start of any relationship.

If the answer is yes to the question of whether Jesus Christ is Lord in his life, then this qualifies as a good foundation for "Christian" friendship. This being established in the beginning, the friendship is open to possibly be extended to courtship or serious relationship. In Amos 3:3, the question was asked, "Can two walk together, except they be agreed?" There has to be a great level of agreement when it comes to friendships as well. If one person is walking with the spirit of God inside of him or her and the other is not, it breaks the boundaries of agreement.

The prophet Amos spoke against the children of Israel because of their idolatrous ways. Whatever you bow down to or give all your attention to, you make that your god. Whatever you put before the one who created you, you make that your god. Whether it is your money, your job, your children and family, or your houses, land, and cars, if it is more important than the manufacturer who created it all, you have made it your god. These are idolatrous ways that are displeasing to the Lord God our maker. So bowing down to and settling for someone who does not know your God, does not want to know your God, or gives you a lame story about how he was baptized as an infant and that is all he needs, is wrong. I promise you, he is in need of some more help. God *knows* exactly who He has created for you. Do not expect anyone who disrespects your God and ignores your desires to treat you like the queen or king that you are.

God told the children of Israel through the prophet Amos in chapter 3 verse 2, "You only have I known of all the families of the earth." In the Amplified version of the Bible as stated in verses 2 and 3, "You only have I known [chosen, sympathized with, and loved] of all the families of the earth; therefore I will visit upon you all your wickedness and punish you for all your iniquities. Do two walk together except they make an appointment and have agreed? Can you continue in a friendship of another who does not love what your God loves and hates what your God hates unless you make a point to *agree* upon it?

God was telling his people, "I have known you far beyond a surface knowledge of who I have created you to be, Israel. I have but a special attention and affection toward you, Israel. You are special, unusual, and unique in my sight." This is how friends should go into dealings with one another and decide if they want such a connection to exist or not. Get to know each other beyond a surface knowledge. It is the responsibility of both parties to determine the value of the newly established union or come to the agreement that the friendship is here to stay. How you determine your walk and relationship with your God (or god) will determine the type of friends you involve yourself with.

This is why communication is vitally important. Get to know as much as you possibly can about another person before any serious decisions are made. Somewhere along the way, the lines of communication were destroyed between the children of Israel and Jehovah

Jireh, their provider. They were no longer in communion with the Lord. Their relationship with the Lord became strained. The children of Israel became a stiff-necked, hard-headed, ungrateful people. They were not continually mindful of what the Lord had already provided for them. They failed to continually thank God for the ways of escape provided them. The children of Israel worshipped the things of the land more than the creator of the land.

Are You a Friend of God?

The next pages are expressly for women to help them to determine the quality of their choice of friends. This goes for all types of friendships but especially long-term relationship/friendships leading into possible marriage between one woman and one man. The bottom line is this: Any woman who is not worshipping the Lord Jesus Christ as redeemer from sin is worshipping Satan and is in agreement with him, the fallen angel who wanted to be like God. Satan and his imps and cronies were so envious and jealous of God's glory they wanted it for themselves. This is where they erred in a big way. They were ejected from heaven, and fell to the earth, and Satan is currently and consistently seeking glory for himself through those who are not worshipping the Lord Jesus Christ with their whole heart, soul, and mind. In John 4:23 it states, "and now is, when the true worshippers shall worship the Father in spirit and in truth for the Father seeketh such to worship him." However, Satan is searching for those who are *not* worshipping the Lord Jesus Christ in spirit and in truth.

There are no two ways about it; either you are bowing to God, the Lord Jesus Christ, or bowing to Satan. We, as woman, have no room to straddle the fence, nor can we afford *not* to be totally confident and sure of whom we serve. As women, believe it or not, our lives are crucial to the success or failure of so many. As Eve had an ear for the enemy's voice, her allegiance to Satan contributed to her husband's demise. Her poor choices and bad decisions resulted in punishment for all. Women, the conscious decision you make to become involved with an individual who is not serving the Lord Jesus Christ as Lord and Savior of his life, as you are, will lead to the demise and destruction of many. Whether you are aware of the individuals who are affected by your choices or not does not negate the responsibility you have in the outcome.

Here is how the penalty for all was birthed by one of mankind—the Woman, Eve. Something significant happened from the time Eve ate of the tree of knowledge of good and evil until the time she gave it to her husband and he did eat. In that brief moment—split seconds from the crossways of hand to tree, from tree to fruit and from fruit to mouth of Eve, then to mouth of Adam the very appetite of "evil" was downloaded into them with exceptional speediness. Just imagine with me as those who were created not to know evil, but good only, became instantaneously privy to every evil working ever created, which initially and purposely had been hidden from them by God. These deeds and acts were never intended for Adam and Eve to be able to identify with. I can see in my finite mind Eve's mind spinning for a matter of milliseconds—then coming to the conclusion in a split second sharing what was *not* supposed to be touched, taken, broken, or given with her covering, Adam. Between great peace and a catastrophic misfortune, decisions made contribute to the disturbance. In geology this is called a cataclysm—a sudden, violent disturbance, especially of a part of the surface of the earth. Have you made any decisions lately that have "rocked" your world or shaken your foundation, decisions that caused a violent disturbance in your life and the lives of others surrounding you? Women, what do you have hiding in your hearts that the family is accursed because of it? What are you hiding underneath? Is it guilt, shame, or rejection? Women cannot be so unconcerned and undisturbed about the effects on others caused by their own selfish behavior. This stems from the lack of yearning to please *only* the Creator. Instead they choose to try and please other people.

My questions to you are these: What are you eating that has been forbidden to you? What is lodged in your digestive tract, causing uneasiness? What are you being kicked out of because you are trying to be something that you are not, as did Satan? What image are you worshipping that is causing you to be envious and jealous of others? Ask yourself, "What idol gods have I set up in my life?" Are you stuck in your wardrobe, attire, and fancy brand-name labels? Does the substance in your closet determine your worth? Is your appearance your god, making you believe that if everything looks good on the outside, everyone will bypass what your heart is actually wearing? Looking to belongings and possessions to fulfill who you are is dangerous. The direction of the heart should be your supreme focus. Do not continue to dress up the "outer" you—your shell, your covering, your container—and ignore the inside contents of the vessel, which is the heart.

The heart must have on love, joy, peace, goodness, gentleness, meekness, temperance, long-suffering, and faith. If we are supposed to live in the Spirit, we should also walk in the Spirit (Galatians 5:22, 25–26 KJV). Do not desire vain, hopeless, futile glory. In other words, it is fine for us ladies to take great care and concern in our appearance, but not to the point it overwhelms and becomes the primary essence of our being. You are *not* the bag you carry; you are *not* the name on the inside of your shoe. Your name is *not* the name on the tag of your suit. All the credit belongs to the maker, just as you belong to your maker, because of the price you were purchased with by the blood of Jesus. Remember that you are not your own. Be sure that you do not become fashion icons *only*, allowing your heart to decay with envy, strife, and contentiousness, turning bitter and wicked. God is looking not on the outer appearance of mankind, but on the heart. The Bible says in John 4:23, God is seeking for a true worshipper, one who worships him in spirit and in truth. We do not want to be those who worship and know not what. John 4:23 reads:

> *But the hour cometh, and now is, when the true worshippers shall worship the Father in spirit and in truth: for the Father seeketh such to worship him.*

Running in Love and Falling for Nothing

When we truly drop everything and run with the *love* of *the giver and sustainer* of life, he smiles and honors what he created for His glory. When this practice takes place, it will not grieve Him that he made us. To fall in love with the creator and begin to worship him because we belong to him is the very reason and essence of our existence. We have been created to show forth *HIS* glory while here on earth. We have been created, shaped, and formed to worship the creator and to make an invisible God visible. In Matthew 22:37–38 it says,

Jesus said unto him, Thou shalt love the Lord thy God with all thy heart, and with all thy soul, and with all thy mind.

This is the first and greatest commandment.

Loving the Lord thy God with all thy heart, soul and mind is beneficial to us. This is the correct and only way to respond to God's love. In responding to God's love correctly, anyone who steps your way requesting a friendship or relationship who loves *not* your God will be easily identifiable only when you are in *this* place yourself. There will be no second-, third-, or fourth-guessing when you are one who shares a personal relationship with the Lord and imitates the character of God in your personality.

Does anyone contending for a prize not expect an award after winning the race? Do you run your race of life for nothing? Do you fall for whatever is put before you, or do you take the time to investigate the package? Women, you have to do your homework and investigate the male package—if you do not, you will fall for anything. Falling denotes to drop, to go down, to descend, to plunge or plummet, to reduce, to decrease, or to collapse. Do you descend or go down into love? Do you plunge or plummet into love? Do you decrease who you are to be in a place called love? Well, when you "fall in love," that is exactly what is done. When you do not take the time to know, observe, and become acquainted with another, you will "fall" for anything, anyone…just something that can stand on two feet. A lover can have all the stuff you desire but merely exist as an attractive candy wrapper with no contents inside. There is no substance on the inside to determine his worth, just an empty package.

God does not want for us to fall for the enemy's tricks and tactics any longer. God wants to be your true love. He wants your undivided attention and time. He wants you to know *HIS* voice like no other.

Do not love yourself and your stuff so much that you forget the One who created you. Do not love the provision given to you so much that you forget God is the one who made the house, the car, and the job and gave you the talent and abilities. God is the one who formed you in His image and after His likeness.

Worshipping God, the Lord Jesus Christ, positions you to receive from the creator the desires of your heart. You do not worship Him for things, but you worship God because you recognize you *exist* only because *He is*. He is the Alpha and Omega, the beginning and the end. He is the author and the finisher of your faith.

When your focus, attention, and desires begin to become centered on how the Creator responds to you and not how everyone and everything else responds to you, then your life becomes a great walk of peace and calmness with satisfaction because of your relationship with the Lord. It displays great joy and great strength because your desires have become exclusively to please the Lord.

The problem is that women do not truly love and value themselves the way they should but instead are living with defense (coping) mechanisms on a daily basis. When you love yourself the right way, you can surely be loved the right way. You may ask, how do you love yourself the right way? How do you know what is right? I am so glad that you asked. No matter what situations you have endured, there is an unquenchable love from God that will accept you, cleanse you, cradle you, and rock you in His arms when you thought no one could ever truly care. His love will overtake you and replace the old with the love of Jesus to make you whole and new again. Give your entire heart to the Lord, and he will mend, repair, and restore you back to the state of completeness. But remember, your completeness is only in Him. We are totally incomplete on our own. When you do not acknowledge the One who fashioned, formed, and produced you, you will spend countless days falling and failing, trying to figure out your purpose and the principle meaning of your life.

You may have a yearning to connect to what we like to call a "soul mate." We must keep in mind, again, that the world's idea of a soul mate is opposite the Christian understanding of a soul mate. The world's expectation of soul mates is two people who are so precisely harmonized that they have everything it takes to maintain a healthy, loving relationship without working at it. Some of the worldliest individuals think that they do not have to work hard for anything, even relationships. They feel it should just happen. This reflects a spirit of entitlement. Anything worth having is worth working for. As stated earlier in the chapter, the world's perspective deals strictly with lustful desires rather than relations built on true love. The world's view of soul mates derives from the lust of the flesh, the lust of the eyes, and the pride of life. 1 John 2:15–17 states,

Love not the world, neither the things that
are in the world. If any man love the world,
the love of the Father is not in him.

For all that is in the world, the lust of the flesh,
and the lust of the eyes, and the pride of life,
is not of the Father, but is of the world.

And the world passeth away, and the lust thereof:
but he that doeth the will of God abideth for ever.

The soul of a man by biblical definition is that part of man that contains the mind, the will, and the emotions. The soul is how we know and identify a person—their personality, their likes and dislikes. We also can identify with their personal uniqueness. The soul is in communication with the human spirit.

You do not find fullness or completeness through finding a soul mate, but truth be told, you will never experience the totality of who you are without the wholesome connection to the One who gave your life. No other man on earth can complete your purpose, only God. Whatever God decides to add to your life thereafter completely depends on the relationship you already have established with Him on your own, not through a soul mate. Let me say it this way: When you have surrendered your mind, will, and emotions to the Lord God, through Jesus Christ, this is how God knows and identifies with you. He knows everything there is to know about you. Why? God has created your personal uniqueness for His glory and His honor. God knows exactly what is good for your life and what has no right to be in your life.

No man on earth will ever give you the soundness and security of who you are or who you are supposed to be. You do not become whole once you meet your soul mate; you should be whole in the Lord before he *finds* you, and this can only happen if you are hidden.

Whoso findeth a wife findeth a good thing
and obtained favour of the Lord. (Proverbs 18:22)

You should be entire, complete, and intact in your mind, heart, body, and soul before you even think about a Boaz. Your mind should be on the things of the Lord. In 1 Corinthians 7:34 it states,

There is difference also between a wife and
a virgin. The unmarried woman careth for the
things of the Lord, that she may be holy both
in body and in spirit: but she that is married
careth for the things of the world how she may
please her husband.

There is no divided allegiance as an unmarried woman or a virgin woman. So, single, saved, celibate, virgin, sold-out-for-Jesus women, I challenge you to concentrate on the things of the Lord, to please Him first. You are to be found serving the Lord in all that you do. All the people around you should have a good report of you as being a woman of notable character. You never know whom Boaz has inquired or questioned about you. Again, you are supposed to be hidden and not flamboyant and uncouth. As you are waiting for Boaz to "find" you, your account should not come back as someone who has a poor reputation, someone lazy and slothful, or someone who wants to be taken care of by a "Prince Charming" with nothing to contribute to the union. The twenty-first-century term for that is called, "gold digger." This type of approach and way of thinking will not help you find favor with those who are hardworking, dedicated, aspiring, and accomplished.

Looking or Serving? What Are You Doing?

In the book of Ruth, Ruth did not put on her brand-name clothing and prance in the presence of the reapers to see which one would notice her first. She spent her days dedicated to the mother of her deceased husband. Ruth served Naomi's God and followed Naomi's steps. Ruth did not go looking for a kinsman redeemer, but her primary concern was tending to her grieving mother in- law who had lost her husband and two sons, one of whom happened to be Ruth's late husband. Ruth was a thoughtful, unselfish, hardworking, and caring woman. Ruth was dedicated to her position and displayed true altruism toward her mother-in-law. She had an unselfish concern for the well-being of Naomi.

Because of Ruth's devotion to Naomi, her attributes were displayed in all she did—so much so that Boaz inquired of the head servant about Ruth's position as she gleaned in his field. Boaz wanted to know who she was and where she came from. She did not have to dress a certain way to gain attention, nor was she flashy or unseemly. All she did was stay committed to the woman of God and do exactly as she was told. How many of us women are devoted and committed to the Lord and the things of God, doing exactly as he tells us to do? The Lord God should be your first Boaz. Boaz means "in him is strength." All of our strength is in God. Do you not know that you are "nothing" without the Lord? As you make the Lord God your treasure, your first priority, he will then give you the desires of your heart, even the desire to be found by a "Boaz"—but God Almighty has to be your *only* strength. It is an honor and a privilege to spend undivided, uninterrupted devotion and dialogue with the Lord. Stay loyal and dedicated to the Lord. Continue to seek his face for the direction He has for your life and remain a stranger to as many potential Boazes as possible. If you are ready, he will find you. You do not have to date every man who pays you a compliment; compliments should already sound familiar to you because of the relationship you already should have with the Lord. Does the Lord tell you that you are the apple of his eye, that you are precious and beautiful in His sight? He will if you put Him first in your life and allow Him to be your strength.

Ruth found favor in the sight of Boaz because she was caught doing the right thing when she thought no one was looking.

Are you continuing in holiness as you wait in servitude to the Lord? Are you remaining anonymous to your earthly Boaz? It is so important to be emptied out before the Lord in your longing to be married. If you are not a stranger to the Lord, that means he knows about you—he knows your likes and dislikes, your wants, your needs and desires. If your intimacy with the Lord is proper there is a special person he already has designed especially for you.

About Boaz

The attributes and character of Boaz are described throughout the second chapter of the book of Ruth. Boaz's qualities and traits define and shape who he is. If you pay close attention, you will find him to be kind, generous, a protector, a leader as well as a provider. The word of God states in Proverbs 18:22,

> *Whoso findeth a wife findeth a good thing,*
> *and obtaineth favour of the Lord.*

At some point in the life of a woman, you want the favor of God attached to your life. You want favor to find you, not flaky to find you. Boaz will already know many details about you that you did not volunteer yourself. He has his way of finding you out, protecting you, providing for you, and even instructing anyone else interested to stay far away from you. He has claimed you as his own, and you have not a clue. This is all done without your knowledge.

Ruth 2:4, Boaz realized there was a new servant working in his vineyard. Upon his arrival, Boaz greeted all the harvesters and blessed them. One characteristic of Boaz, according to the book of Ruth, was that he was kind and respectful.

And, behold Boaz came from Bethlehem and
said unto the reapers, The Lord be with you.
And they answered him, The Lord bless thee.

Boaz had servants but showed kindness and decency toward them and did not treat them as second-class citizens. Boaz knew his position and his power along with his authority and continued to remain humane toward those who did not have what he had.

Another attribute of Boaz is that of being acutely aware of his surroundings and keeping count of what belongs to him. He asked a question to the reaper in charge, as is written Ruth 2:5 saying,

Then said Boaz unto his servant that was
set over the reapers, Whose damsel is this?

Boaz was all about the business. He identified a new face in the crowd. He noticed an unfamiliar face that was not accounted for in his record keeping. Boaz was a businessman. Ruth 2:8-9 explains the stance of Boaz.

So Boaz said to Ruth, "My daughter, listen to me.
Do not go and glean in another field
and do not go away from here. Stay here
with the women who work for me.

Watch the field where the men are
harvesting, and follow along after the women.
I have told the men not to lay a hand on you.
And whenever you are thirsty, go and get
a drink from the water jars the men
have filled." (NIV)

Boaz did not want to see a high-quality worker such as Ruth discontented in her work. He insisted she not go away, but rather stay as if she was one of the hired servants. He instructed her where to go to receive portions of the harvest designed by his own hand. He not only appreciated her hard work in his field but also the dedication she displayed to her mother-in-law. Boaz took great notice of Ruth and admired her worth and her value.

Women, "your" Boaz will appreciate you before he even gets to know who you are. He will set it up for you to be blessed that not only God is working on your behalf, but Boaz is preparing himself for you, too.

Ruth was surprised how kind Boaz was to her, a foreigner and a stranger. In Ruth 2:10 it states,

Then she fell on her face, and bowed herself to the ground, and said unto him, Why have I found grace in thine eyes, that thou shouldest take knowledge of me, seeing I am a stranger.

Ladies, do not be astonished or shocked when your Boaz finds you out. If you are living a life of holiness, serving the way God has called you to serve and being about your Father's business, you should "expect" Boaz to approach you. But do not become sly and cunning to do works in hopes that someone spots you. Your efforts will be totally in vain because a Boaz knows how to spot a Ruth and can smell phony miles away.

His reply was as follows,

Boaz replied, "I've been told all about what you have done for your mother-in-law since the death of your husband. (Ruth 2:11)

Boaz let Ruth know he had been watching her all along. He spoke blessings over her life. Boaz prayed that the Lord would repay her richly for what she had done.

Now let us bring it up to speed to the twenty-first century. A "modern-day" Boaz is not confused about who he is. He is not seeking for his purpose and position in life. He already knows who he is. A modern-day Boaz in not confused about his sexuality. He believes and walks in Leviticus 18:22.

You shall not lie with a man as with a woman;
it is an abomination. (Amplified)

Do not have sexual relations with a man as
one does with a woman, this is detestable. (NIV)

He is not making excuses or compromises about his moral convictions, which are backed up by the word of God. He is content in the skin he is in.

In Matthew 22:37–38 it says,

Jesus said unto him, Thou shalt love the Lord
thy God with all thy heart, and with all thy soul,
and with all thy mind.

This is the first and greatest commandment.

Ladies, all I am saying is this: Love the Lord God with all thy heart, all thy soul, and thy entire mind, and tell every male species trying to step to you with two left feet (incorrectly) whom your Father is. He has to approach you with respect, kindness, generosity, and integrity. Are these not the very same traits your heavenly Father has been demonstrating to you all along? If you have not received this kind of treatment with your heavenly Father yet, your focal point is misaligned and out of kilter. Why would God send you your lifelong mate if you are a jagged, broken piece of glass? You will cut him into raggedy, small pieces if he ever tried to comfort or embrace you in times of need.

Ruth and Boaz are used as a type of simile the way the Lord desires you to have a relationship with Him. God wants us to serve him with all of our heart, all of our mind and with everything we have in us. The natural Boaz is important, but not as significant as our Spiritual Boaz, Jesus Christ our Lord and Savior is first and foremost. He is the primary care giver, the first lover and the only keeper of our souls.

Once I began to realize who I was and who the Lord God created me to be in Him, only then could I relinquish all of my desires, all of my expectations and all of my needs and wants to the Lord. As I began to fall deeper in love with the Lord and my desire to continually be in His peaceful presence, the more content and satisfied with my life I became. As I immersed myself in prayer, meditation and studying of the word of God, the less stressed, concerned and worried I became about most situations and circumstances. I noticed as my heart, my love, my peace and my desires were totally focused and pointed toward the Lord, He had my natural Boaz (Michael) watching, studying and preparing a new life with him while I was with the Lord.

So I end with this: *Don't settle* for less than God's very best for your life. Get to know the Lord Jesus Christ in your virginity, your singleness, and your abstinence. His knowledge is inexhaustible, unlimited, and infinite, and He loves you the *right way*!

Remember:

1 Corinthians 2:9

But as it is written, Eye hath not seen, nor ear heard, neither have entered into the heart of man, the things which God hath prepared for them that love him.

Made in the USA
Columbia, SC
24 June 2021